PRAISE FOR
HOLISTIC LEADERSHIP

Many organizations fail to treat DEIB as a priority because they are unfamiliar with it and uncomfortable with it. There is no uniformly accepted road map or best practice for converting DEIB principles into practice.

Using clear language and an intentionally sequential approach, *Holistic Leadership* shows how to lead systemic change by educating an organization about how to connect its value systems, behaviors, workplace expectations, and practices to the Principles of DEIB.

As President of the Diversity and Inclusion Professionals of Central Pennsylvania, which the authors co-founded, I have seen the lasting effects of their approach to DEIB. Members from a wide array of organizations have embraced the concepts explained in *Holistic Leadership* and are using its "how to" lessons learned to improve their effectiveness.

I have no doubt that *Holistic Leadership* is destined to become a much relied upon resource among our membership and organizations across the country.

—Rev. Ruth Moore
Director, Community Relations, Diversity Equity & Inclusion –
Penn State Health – Pennsylvania Psychiatric Institute

As a gay community college president who has committed his life's work as a college leader to advancing Diversity, Equity, Inclusion, and Belonging (DEIB), I found *Holistic Leadership* to be both practical and visionary. It directly confronts the performative, surface-level DEIB efforts that too often fail to drive meaningful progress, offering instead a strategic and systemic framework grounded in organizational self-awareness and true cultural transformation.

What resonates most is the book's commitment to meeting institutions where they are—recognizing their unique histories, leadership structures, levels of readiness, and the deeply entrenched realities of institutional and systemic racism and homophobia. This tailored, honest approach is especially critical in higher education, where aligning DEIB with mission, values, and student success is not just important—it is imperative.

Holistic Leadership doesn't just provide tools; it equips educational leaders with the mindset, language, and strategy needed to dismantle barriers and embed equity into the very fabric of institutional life. It is essential reading for anyone serious about breaking the chains of systemic oppression in education and building a truly inclusive culture of belonging.

—John J. "SKI" Sygielski, M.B.A., Ed.D.
President and CEO, HACC, Central Pennsylvania's Community College

Having collaborated with Frank for many years, I can personally attest to his unwavering passion and dedication to the principles and practices outlined in this work. His pragmatic approach to fostering welcoming and inclusive environments has always been evident. *Holistic Leadership* particularly shines in its "meet them where they are" philosophy, effectively addressing the operational realities companies face in this space. Rather than imposing initiatives that an organization may not fully grasp or be prepared for, the authors present a process that begins at an organization's current stage, guiding it toward creating an environment where all team members feel welcomed and supported.

Holistic Leadership stands apart from any other leadership book I have encountered. It compellingly argues why all leaders must embrace the perspective, as Mr. Hershey so aptly put it, that "business is a matter of human service."

—John Lawn
President and CEO, Hershey Entertainment & Resorts Company

In their enlightening book, *Holistic Leadership*, Deborah D. Vereen, CCDP/AP, and Frank Miles, Esq., present a remarkably engaging and practical approach to leadership development. Drawing from their unique experiences, Deborah's extensive background in business and DEIB initiatives, combined with Frank's sharp legal expertise, provides an insightful and grounded perspective that resonates deeply with today's leaders. The authors artfully emphasize the significance of cultivating a culture of belonging through sequential, holistic, and systemic change, offering a timely and invaluable contribution to the discourse on leadership in the current political environment. Leaders striving to navigate the complexities of the modern workplace, empower critical thinking, and foster truly inclusive cultures will discover a wealth of strategies and resources within these pages. Moreover, Vereen and Miles are passionately committed to creating environments where individuals not only thrive, but organizations also achieve lasting success. This book is an essential guide for anyone eager to elevate their leadership journey and make a lasting impact in their organization.

—Diane M. Crawford, M.Ed.
Executive Director Institutional Culture,
Whitman School of Management Syracuse University

As a leader at an organization that is committed to the Principles of DEIB, *Holistic Leadership* enhanced both my ability to integrate those principles into my planning and how I carry out my responsibilities. It also informs how I explain to others why these Principles are so important to achieving our objectives as an educational institution.

Working with Frank in my previous position, I saw firsthand how important it is to develop savvy organizational intelligence—one of the key components of the Holistic Leadership approach—to garner support for initiatives from the decision-makers and influencers able to make them a reality.

For leaders at any level, *Holistic Leadership* is a must-read. It not only challenges you to rethink the way you lead but also offers the clarity and resources needed to create a truly inclusive and thriving workplace where everyone can belong and grow.

—David Curry
Director, Center for Career Exploration and Development, Ithaca College

Holistic Leadership presents a framework that is rooted in the critical question of whether an organization's commitment is merely verbal or consistently demonstrated. It offers clarity, courage, and a tested path forward.

Holistic Leadership affirms a truth every DEIB practitioner must hold: We are called to meet institutions where they are yet must be wise enough to know when the ground is fertile for change and when it is not. This is more than strategy; it is a safeguard for a practitioner's integrity, resilience, and purpose.

By translating vision into the language and culture of each organization, this approach moves DEIB from aspiration to sustainable action, empowering practitioners to discern not only *how* to advance, but also *when* to go, and when to let go.

—Dr. Felicia Brown-Haywood, LPC, NCC, M.Div.
Retired Higher Education Administrator/Inclusive Excellence Practitioner

Many HR leaders and executives struggle to advance DEIB beyond checklists and isolated trainings. What's often missing is a clear, practical plan for creating lasting cultural change. *Holistic Leadership* fills that gap. Using simple language and a step-by-step approach, the authors show how to align organizational values, behaviors, and workplace practices with the core Principles of Diversity, Equity, Inclusion, and Belonging.

As an HR leader, I sincerely appreciate the book's emphasis on meeting organizations where they are while still holding a vision for progress. It is not about theory; it is about actionable strategies that leaders at any stage can implement to foster dignity, safety, and belonging. *Holistic Leadership* is a resource I will return to often and one I believe every HR professional should have at hand as we work to build stronger, more inclusive organizations.

—Candice N. Rice SHRM-SCP
Director of Human Resources, Orthopedic Institute of PA

Deborah Vereen and Frank Miles are leaders in DEIB and more importantly believe that successful organizations have DEIB interwoven into their organizational cultures.

Over their careers in corporate America, they have found successful organizations' DEIB initiatives are naturally interwoven into organizational cultures. It's effortless and natural.

Deborah and Frank focus on core values, relationships, the way we relate with each other, our customers and competitors. Given the increasing diversity of our nation and a truly global economy, it's an evolutionary process, but it's the future, and it's critical to successful organizations.

Their book is a positive, helpful guide for organizations to become better, building better workplace cultures that contribute to tomorrow's success.

—David Black
President and CEO (ret.), Harrisburg Regional Chamber of Commerce

Holistic Leadership is going to be the "GO TO BOOK," your own encyclopedia of DEIB knowledge. It will be your reference for clear concise answers to the questions that you did not want to raise your hand and ask because you were afraid or embarrassed to ask, but you needed the honest answers.

I was a HR professional who thought I knew this subject but after attending seminars and discussions presented by these authors I realized how little I actually knew. I was fortunate enough to be open minded to accept these practices through a different lens. Now I am like a sponge anxiously awaiting more knowledge.

The content is relatable to a new hire recruiter as well as a company president. The concepts are different from most of the books I had read on these subjects. There is no question left unanswered because you will begin to see a different perspective.

I now have a different lens than most HR professionals because of my exposure to REAL DEIB practitioners who live and breathe equality.

This book will be your investment to your career longevity.

—Evelyn Kenley
Ahold USA HR Professional (ret.)

By providing a roadmap for approaching leadership holistically, the authors clarify how to align DEIB with the organization's mission and goals in this very effective educational resource guide. Rather than stepping away from DEIB, Vereen and Miles emphasize the urgency of continuing the work, so it becomes a part of the organization's DNA, thus the importance of DEIB is never in question.

Holistic Leadership should be referenced by every current and future leaders as they guide their organizations toward future success.

—**Pamela J Smith, Ed.D.**
Adjunct Professor Business, Muskegon Community College

Leadership and the components of leadership have always been analyzed, debated, and discussed. DEIB has taken its place as a part of these debates. DEIB, as a discipline of leadership, has always been an evolving social economic science. DEIB has always manifested itself based on an ever-evolving and perpetually changing mixture of the environment, human mental acuity, attitude, and human psyche. It has been characterized by DEIB professionals and practitioners as a perpetual "work-in-progress" that will always have a profound effect and impact on the effectiveness of any organization.

The authors of *Holistic Leadership* have "lived the experience" of identifying and solving the challenges of DEIB in organizations, companies, governments, and the academic community.

Their experience, education, and training has made them well known and sought after experts in the leadership/DEIB space. Their concept of leadership and how the Principles of DEIB and leadership are inevitably intertwined will make an undeniable impact on the effectiveness of any organization. After years of collective experiences, these two brilliant minds have decided to collaborate on writing *Holistic Leadership*, addressing how and why this concept could be effectively integrated into the very fabric of any organization and/or company.

This book demonstrates and definitively shows how the Principles of DEIB must be tracked and monitored just like any other discipline of an organization and/or company. By doing so, it puts an organization into a constant mode of continuous learning, thus an organization is inevitably constantly in a mode of continuous improvement. If the organization is committed to digesting these learnings, while remaining unbiased, and turning these learnings into transformative policies, procedures, and practices, it should be successful in running an effective organization.

Holistic Leadership does this by not just quoting the obvious of what your desired outcome will be, but more importantly, this book tells you *how* you get to the desired outcome.

Holistic Leadership will be one of the leaders in the development and implementation of concepts and effective tools in the "how to" guide for developing effective leadership within the leadership/DEIB space for years to come.

—Henry H. Edwards
Vice President (ret.), Organizational Effectiveness, Royal Ahold Delhaize N.V.;
Executive Director and Founder of The Entrepreneurship and Leadership
Institute (ELI) at Howard University

ENDORSEMENTS FROM CUSTOMERS OF THE VEREEN GROUP

After Attending Holistic Leadership Discovery Learnings

Speaking in front of others can be simple; but being a change maker, both motivating and empowering people, takes work. Thank you so much for being our keynote speaker. You brought so much value and information to everyone and helped create an enabling environment for learning. We hope you know your impact on others doesn't go unnoticed.

—Community Action Association DEI Summit Keynote

The DEI Workshop was excellent, I learned so much. It was from an aspect which I had not really heard before and really spoke to my work in government. I also really appreciate her approach to the work of DEI as a statewide organization. THANK YOU for the opportunity.

**—Statewide Nonprofit Community Organization
Board of Directors**

Thank you so much for your great session last week with Diversity and Inclusion Professionals of Central PA (DIPCPA). I found it moving and helpful. I really appreciate the level of personal accountability you ask people to bring to this work, and I also really appreciated the time to consider my "DEI End in Mind." I have been thinking about it ever since. I am so glad that we are partnering with you. Thank you for teaching us how to do this work more effectively.

—**Statewide Cyber Charter School**

Ms. Vereen's presentation is the most cogent, useful, and effective presentation on the issue of workforce diversity that I have ever heard . . . and that includes twenty-five years or more in the working world when the diversity issue was women in management positions in marketing.

—**D. Rudd, Chairman, Dept. of Business, (ret.)**
Lebanon Valley College

Absolutely fantastic! Deborah, you are a gift to people everywhere. Thank you for your kind, thoughtful, and heartfelt leadership this evening.

—**Health Care DEI Summit**

You were absolutely incredible. You left us speechless (in a great way). You were impactful, approachable, thought-provoking, and informative. I learned (and identified some things I need to "unlearn") today! We can't say enough about how phenomenal your keynote presentation was.

—**Health Care Town Hall**

Just a follow-up, I have talked so much about your training. You are always so amazing at bringing the business case to everything. Somehow you always take the emotional piece out of it and make things seem so sensible! Thank you, I look forward to continued connections!

—**Chamber of Commerce Board of Directors**
DEIB Discovery Learning

Thank you so much for the training today. It was excellent. I am looking forward to the next time we are together.

—**CPA Accounting Firm**

Excellent speaker; the speaker was very well prepared and knowledgeable about the topic. Very engaging. This speaker/presentation was priceless. Great presenter, very useful information. Deborah was great! Awesome. Excellent. Excellent presentation!

—**Evaluation Comments from Society for Human Resources**
Management (SHRM) Chapter Meeting Presentation

Wow, as I looked at your session overview topics, I'm reminded why your presentation is so powerful. I might add that's a view shared by everyone who has attended UGI University (high potential management). Your session has been one of our highest-rated sessions by attendees, which is pretty remarkable.

—**USA and 17 European Countries Public Utility**

HOLISTIC
LEADERSHIP

HOLISTIC

How to Weave
Diversity, Equity,
Inclusion & Belonging
Principles into Your
Organization's
DNA

LEADERSHIP

Deborah D. Vereen, CCDP/AP
Frank Miles, Esq.

PYP **Publish** Your Purpose

For permission requests, write to the publisher, addressed "Attention: Permissions Coordinator," at the address below.

Publish Your Purpose
141 Weston Street, #155
Hartford, CT, 06141

PYP **Publish** Your Purpose

The opinions expressed by the Author are not necessarily those held by Publish Your Purpose.

Ordering Information: Quantity sales and special discounts are available on quantity purchases by corporations, associations, and others. For details, contact the author at dvereen@thevereengroup.com.

Edited by: Dana Micheli
Cover design by: Rebecca Pollock
Typeset by: Medlar Publishing Solutions Pvt Ltd., India

ISBN: 979-8-88797-202-2 (hardcover)
ISBN: 979-8-88797-203-9 (paperback)
ISBN: 979-8-88797-204-6 (ebook)

Library of Congress Control Number: 2025913750

First edition, January 2026.

Publish Your Purpose is a hybrid publisher of nonfiction books. Our mission is to elevate the voices often excluded from traditional publishing. We intentionally seek out authors and storytellers with diverse backgrounds, life experiences, and unique perspectives to publish books that will make an impact in the world. Do you have a book idea you would like us to consider publishing? Please visit PublishYourPurpose. com for more information.

TABLE OF CONTENTS

PART 3: TOOLS FOR MOVING FORWARD

PREFACE

The Why of This Book

The subject of a nonfiction book, what it's about, is nearly always evident from its title. But the *Why* of a book—the authors' motivation for creating a written narrative of their perspective—provides important context for the reader, lending a perspective that enhances understanding of the content.

Our *Why* in co-authoring *Holistic Leadership* is the realization of a long-time objective: the advancement of meaningful, systemic change in the workplace by helping organizations weave the Principles of DEIB (Diversity, Equity, Inclusion, Belonging) into their cultural DNA. The catalyst for writing this book came from a group of DEIB professionals who asked us to teach them how to effectuate change.

Organizations continue to recognize DEIB efforts as integral to business survival and long-range success. Many realize, as do we, that DEIB is not just the right thing to do; it is the smart, proactive, strategic approach for forward-thinking, growth-minded organizations. However, while the *will* is there, the *way* to do so successfully often remains elusive. Such was the case with this group of DEIB professionals and their respective employers.

The key, we have learned, is to use a pragmatic, business-oriented strategy that meets an organization at its current level of understanding of DEIB. We counsel an approach that fosters receptivity and sustainability.

Many of the DEIB professionals told us how ill-prepared they were for this work. Often, they lacked any experience or training in the discipline, having held unrelated positions before management tapped them to lead Diversity efforts across the organization. For some, it was the first time their employer had even openly acknowledged the need for such efforts.

Though unsure of what the term Diversity means or its importance for their enterprise, leaders nevertheless sensed that they needed to do something to address it—whatever "it" is. They were seeing articles and seminars about it everywhere, as "Diversity" and related terminology had entered the vernacular of business, education, and government. "Equity," "Inclusion," and "Belonging" eventually became part of that language as well, but to those just getting started on the journey, an appreciation for the nuances of DEIB terminology was still a long way off.

Moreover, many Diversity Directors and those in similar roles—regardless of their experience or their organization's level of awareness around Diversity—expressed deep frustration with the agonizingly slow pace of progress. Though they worked across a variety of industries and at very different companies, educational institutions, and government entities, they experienced a seeming inability to advance even the most modest DEIB initiatives. It wasn't long before a common cause of their frustration emerged.

In their haste to show support for Diversity, most organizations neglect to educate themselves about DEIB or seek out individuals with experience in implementing DEIB strategies. Since Diversity appears to them to be about the workforce, organizations frequently delegate responsibility for "making their organization diverse" to the Human Resources Department. Others assume that demonstrating Diversity means highlighting the involvement of Persons of Color. They created Diversity Departments and routinely put a Person of Color in charge.

As mentioned, the new Diversity Director often lacks DEIB experience; they also, in many cases, do not have much authority, let alone a budget. Yet leadership, when asked about their commitment to Diversity, is now able to point to their Diversity Department. They had checked the Diversity box, or so they thought.

Over the course of two sessions attended by more than ninety DEIB professionals, we mapped out the key elements of a DEIB strategic framework that we had successfully implemented at our respective companies. (These were, in fact, the same elements we had advised others to embrace when creating their own framework.) Before doing so, however, we tackled critical questions which all those in the DEIB discipline need to ask: "Do I have the courage to do this work? And, if so, am I willing to put in the effort necessary—including understanding the history of the United States as seen through a DEIB lens, and committing to ongoing learning about the evolution of DEIB—to ensure that I am prepared?"

We then addressed that principal source of frustration for those working in DEIB: an inability to effectuate systemic change at their respective organizations. Time and again, we heard questions and comments that revealed a lack of Organizational Intelligence.

For one thing, several DEIB professionals could not articulate what was important to their organization. Nor did they fully understand how decisions were made—that is, who had real power and who were influencers. Assuming that titles and reporting responsibilities limited their ability to navigate within the entire entity, they were frequently stymied in their attempts to move DEIB initiatives forward.

A generational difference among DEIB professionals also began to surface during these sessions. We found that many from newer generations, such as Millennials and Generation Z, had little patience for working within the existing framework of their organization, especially those dominated by members of the Boomer Generation (in most cases, older White males). Moreover, they felt that the case for increased Diversity, greater Equity, and the creation of an inclusive environment was so compelling and self-evident that those in power *should* recognize it and readily embrace change.

Indeed, many were restive as we explained the importance of meeting people where they are in order to bring them along on the DEIB journey. We counseled reasonable (not inexhaustible) patience in their efforts to translate DEIB concepts into terms that decision-makers could understand and strategies they could see as valuable.

Ultimately, we laid out our vision of how employees with DEIB responsibilities (be they individual contributors or in the position of Chief Diversity Officers, Chief Equity Officers, Chief Culture Officers, or similar roles) can break through the well-established, but generally unacknowledged, challenges and barriers that prevent many companies from achieving real change, no matter how genuine their intentions. While not a simple, one-size-fits-all plan, this vision is centered upon several core concepts that readily translate across all organizations, large and small, public or private, for profit or non-profit.

Over time, we saw that many aspects of our approach can also be employed by members of an organization who, though not DEIB professionals, share the commitment to the Principles of DEIB. We would, therefore, include these allies in the collective we call "DEIB Leaders."

Ultimately, we authored this book for the same reason we co-founded an organization dedicated to DEIB professionals[1] in 2008: to assist these brave leaders as they work to create and implement policies, practices, and initiatives that move organizations forward in the quest for genuine equality in the United States. We believe in sharing lessons learned, and in the pages that follow we endeavor to start you on a path to becoming a successful, forward-looking DEIB Leader.

---

[1] The Diversity and Inclusion Professionals of Central Pennsylvania. DIPCPA.org.

INTRODUCTION

A Tested New Way of Thinking About DEIB

The fact that you're reading this book likely means that you've had some exposure to the acronyms DEI or DEIB. Maybe you're a DEIB Professional or an employee who was required to attend "Diversity Training." Perhaps the media has been the primary source of that exposure. Whatever your experience with DEIB, be it personal or based on the opinions of others, we assure you that it is different from what we offer here.

While many organizations have undertaken DEIB initiatives, too many present a one-size-fits-all approach that fails to consider each organization's unique history and character. It is time for a new way of thinking—a holistic approach and process that weaves the Principles and practices of authentic DEIB into the fabric of organizations across the country. Systemic structural change is the keystone to achieving America's promise of genuine equality.

Holistic Leadership presents that approach. It explains why and *how* this can be accomplished by leveraging Organizational Intelligence to meet an organization at its current understanding of DEIB, foster receptivity, and bring it forward. Our most significant innovations are:

HOLISTIC AND SYSTEMIC

Over our combined fifty-plus years of experience, we have discerned that the failure to align DEIB practices with an organization's mission, vision, values, and strategic objectives is the single greatest reason initiatives flounder or disappear. We show how to identify what an organization cares about and provide insights about connecting the dots so its decision-makers can understand the short- and long-term value of DEIB.

Most organizations struggle with DEIB because they don't understand how to make it part of what they do and how they do it. Our holistic approach teaches that DEIB Principles must be implemented strategically and sequentially. We explain the preparation required *before* beginning or continuing the DEIB journey.

MEETING THEM WHERE THEY ARE

Rather than taking the predominant approach—that of prematurely pushing off the shelf DEIB initiatives that an organization may think it needs but doesn't fully understand or is not ready for—we advocate meeting them where they are with their current perspective. This is where the creation of a path that fosters receptiveness (lowers the wall) begins, building upon their existing foundation of knowledge and experience so the organization can understand, digest, and leverage the Principles of DEIB and move forward.

INTEGRATION OF ORGANIZATIONAL INTELLIGENCE

Many working to advance DEIB Principles cannot articulate what is important to their organization. Nor do they fully understand how decisions are made, that is, who has real power, who has influence, and what that looks like. As a result, they are stymied in their attempts to move DEIB initiatives forward. We explain how to develop Organizational Intelligence and leverage the organization's own brand identity words and priorities to weave DEIB Principles into its culture.

SEQUENCING

Unlike the common practice of selecting from a menu of potential DEIB initiatives in no particular order (a.k.a. throwing spaghetti against the wall to see what sticks), we describe a sequential approach in which an organization must reach certain destinations before it can move on to the next. There are ample resources articulating the need for and benefits of DEIB Principles, but a paucity of instruction for recognizing and implementing them. We explain how to identify the actions that are needed, as well as the order in which they should be executed.

INTERNAL, NOT EXTERNAL

Too many organizations rely upon external consultants to drive their DEIB efforts. We advise that DEIB Principles be learned and adopted from within. To achieve sustainable change, organizations must empower qualified employees to lead them in the systematic implementation of a well-conceived DEIB strategic framework.

SUSTAINABLE, NOT "CHECK THE BOX"

As with the use of external consultants, DEIB initiatives are often unsustainable because they are not organic to the organization. Many organizations and their leaders default to a check the box mentality, with highly visible "quick wins" (a.k.a. low-hanging fruit) or "one-offs" like cultural awareness events.

Without a coherent, holistic approach that the whole organization understands, its DEIB efforts are destined to be ineffective. In the pages that follow you'll learn how our systematic and sequential approach weaves DEIB Principles into an organization's method of operation now and for the future.

In Part 1, we clarify what authentic DEIB is and what it is not, thereby tackling misconceptions that have undermined the public's appreciation for the value of DEIB.

Part 2 addresses why so many DEIB initiatives fail, and how to avoid these missteps. Most importantly, we show you how to align DEIB Principles with what is important to your organization, and design sustainable practices to help it achieve its existing objectives and end in mind.

And, because passion for DEIB Principles is not enough to be an effective leader, we devote Part 3 to identifying the tools you need to help your organization move forward. These include Organizational Intelligence, courage with knowledge, and a command of evolving terminology and varied components of changing population demographics.

Whatever your DEIB journey has looked like thus far, and no matter what job title you hold, we invite you to start afresh. Embrace this new way of thinking about DEIB, and you will be better prepared to help your organization advance toward a sustainable culture of Belonging.

PART 1

THE END
IN MIND

CHAPTER 1

AN INCLUSIVE ENVIRONMENT ENABLING A CULTURE OF BELONGING

> Terms included in the Glossary appear in **bold type** the first time they are used.

We believe in providing clarity, so before you dive in, let's connect the dots in this chapter's title to ensure you have a clear understanding of the path's beginning and the travel components to a sustainable **end in mind**. Remember, "Success is a Journey, not a Destination!"

You cannot *make* everyone feel that they are part of an organization's culture. People *know* when they belong or not, when their authentic selves "fit" or not. You must first embrace the **Diversity, Equity,** and **Inclusion** foundational components to establish an Environment of Inclusion that will then enable a **Culture of Belonging** with sustainable demonstrated behaviors. The value and reward come when you systemically and sequentially do the **DEIB** work; people *know* they belong and display authentic ownership in their engagement and performance.

The United States of America is a republic operating as a democracy with a one-of-a-kind and globally admired Constitution. Its top four brand identities are "**Equal/Equality**"; *"E Pluribus Unum"* ("Out of Many, One"); "A Nation of Immigrants"; and "A Government Of the People, By the People, For the People." There are also several popular phrases referencing the United States that create expectations about its core brand.

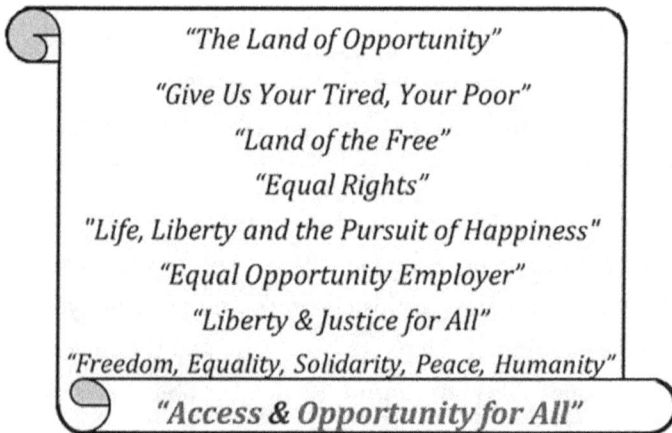

> *"The Land of Opportunity"*
> *"Give Us Your Tired, Your Poor"*
> *"Land of the Free"*
> *"Equal Rights"*
> *"Life, Liberty and the Pursuit of Happiness"*
> *"Equal Opportunity Employer"*
> *"Liberty & Justice for All"*
> *"Freedom, Equality, Solidarity, Peace, Humanity"*
> *"Access & Opportunity for All"*

How is it, then, that the United States, which is approaching its 250th birthday, has not yet achieved Equality for All?!! The answer lies in a pattern that has occurred throughout its history: taking three steps forward, two steps back, and—every forty to sixty years—a *huge* leap backward.

A democracy is fragile and cannot survive without well-informed and responsible citizen engagement. The U.S. democracy is built not only upon the rule of law and the spirit of the law, but also on a social contract that we have with one another to keep and grow our freedoms, rights, and opportunities to thrive.

This contract, often expressed by the phrase *e pluribus unum*, is woven into the fabric of the United States, creating an expectation and accountability to live by. It is its national motto, reminding us that the U.S. is made up of many different people and cultures, but together, We *The People*, form One Nation.

E pluribus unum can be found on the back of the one-dollar bill, specifically in the banner held by the eagle, as well as on all U.S. coinage—the latter, a requirement by law since February 12, 1873. It also appears on the Great Seal of the United States and on the flags and seals of the U.S. Senate and the House of Representatives.

It is well past the time for the United States to catch its North Star, embrace, and live up to its own expectations. A key piece of this—and a national imperative, given the constant evolution of the world— is not only understanding the DEIB (Diversity, Equity, Inclusion, **Belonging**) approach to interacting as human beings, but practicing the Principles of DEIB and its Inclusion Enablers. As recently as 2025 a U.S. Federal Court of Appeals Chief Judge maintained that embracing Diversity acknowledges the country's social identity, fostering Equity opens opportunities for all, and practicing Inclusion creates environments where everyone feels valued, asking rhetorically, "What could be more American than that?"[2]

Our End In Mind is a genuine and sustainable Culture of Belonging is the United States' North Star for tapping into, enhancing, and leveraging creativity, innovation, lived experiences, and critical thinking solutions. Everyone, *all* people, make up U.S. society. Our aim is to establish an environment that not only enables, but fosters, this Culture of Belonging—in essence, to ensure the country lives up to its motto.

THE PRINCIPLES OF DEIB

DEIB is about Humanity: You and Me, All of Us. Its three Principles are straightforward and beneficial to every member of society.

1. All human beings possess multiple **Dimensions of Diversity** and should be *seen* and *valued* for the totality of who they are, not as one or a few specific dimensions.

    • Being *seen* is about the "imbedded Dimensions of Diversity" that are easily perceived by others: Race,

---

[2] National Association Of Diversity Officers In Higher Education, et al., Plaintiffs-Appellees, v. Donald J. Trump, et al., Defendants-Appellants (United States Court Of Appeals for the Fourth Circuit, Slip op. at 5, March 14, 2025). Here is the full paragraph from which this quote is taken: "And despite the vitriol now being heaped on DEI, people of good faith who work to promote Diversity, Equity, and Inclusion deserve praise, not opprobrium. For when this country embraces true Diversity, it acknowledges and respects the social identity of its people. When it fosters true Equity, it opens opportunities and ensures a level playing field for all. And when its policies are truly inclusive, it creates an environment and culture where everyone is respected and valued. What could be more American than that?"

Ethnicity, Hue of Skin, Accent, Gender, Disability, Religion, Height, Weight.

- Being *valued* is about the "authentic Diversity dimensions" that others do not easily perceive without being receptive to engage: knowledge, abilities, lived experience, creativity, and several more.

2. All members of society should treat one another with mutual **respect** and fairness.

   - "Society" includes individuals, as well as government institutions and other organizations comprised of a collection of individuals.

3. Put into practice the three **Inclusion Enablers** of **Civility**, Respect, and **Kindness**.

   - These Enablers should be engrained into the norms of U.S. society.

DEIB APPROACH AND EXPANDING THE TABLE ALIGNMENT

A **holistic approach** teaches that **DEIB Principles** must be implemented strategically and sequentially for sustainable cultural change. This means systematically weaving DEIB Principles into an organization's culture and aligning DEIB practices with its Mission, Vision, Core Values, and Strategic Objectives.

As we move forward, envision what is possible but may not, at present, be seen. Take our lessons learned with you as you start the proven path to becoming a DEIB Leader.

CHAPTER 2

CLARIFYING DEFINITIONS AND MOVING PAST ACRONYMS

Words matter, and nowhere more so than in the discipline of DEIB. One need only reflect on the battles over authentically identifying "**White Privilege**," "Black Lives Matter," and "Critical Race Theory" to recognize that the fight is waged largely over what those words mean.

In fact, more often than not, efforts to have a meaningful dialogue about DEIB and **systemic change** are hampered by misrepresentations and misunderstandings of what acronyms and words stand for. At times, "DEIB" has even been co-opted and used as a weapon against those trying to advance its principles.

The language of DEIB should not and must not be defined by those who lack the knowledge and experience to properly explain it.

To allow that to happen is to condemn the country to repeating the injustices that persist to this day.

The DEIB discipline itself has been subjected to challenges about its name. Not long ago, the word "Diversity" was used to include everything from employee hiring to nearly every concept and program related to race. Gradually, that term began to encompass other characteristics, such as ethnicity, sexual orientation, generations, and socioeconomic status.

Diversity as an objective also began to be misinterpreted as negative, with some claiming that it placed emphasis on differences. Rather than embrace the notion that "a rising tide raises all boats," Diversity was disingenuously recast as another form of **affirmative action** or "**reverse discrimination.**"

In an effort to alleviate this resistance, the terminology was expanded, beginning with the word "Inclusion." The intent was to assure that everyone, including members of the majority group, are part of the journey to genuine inclusiveness. Hopefully, then, we could get on with the business of identifying **barriers** and **challenges** to remedying systemic inequities.

While an improvement, the term "Diversity and Inclusion" ("D&I") was still wanting as a means of conveying the overall objective of the initiatives that fell under this title—that objective being Equity. Indeed, to those resistant to societal change in the name of D&I, it was an attack on individuals—a zero-sum approach in which those in the majority would be replaced by those who are "diverse." Both "Diversity" and "Inclusion" were portrayed as euphemisms for giving advantages to **Persons of Color**: "diverse candidates" were nonwhites; "Inclusion" meant the inclusion of nonwhites.

DEIB is not a numbers game, nor has that ever been the case.

By adding "Equity," the foundational, albeit aspirational, values of fairness and impartiality enshrined in the U.S. Constitution were incorporated into the DEIB lexicon. "Equity" speaks to the condition of society as a whole, not just individuals as compared to other individuals.

The difficulty in establishing a clear definition of DEIB has also been exacerbated by the frequent introduction of other acronyms designed to capture what various groups believe to be the key components of their vision for achieving equality. EDI (Equity, Diversity, and Inclusion); JEDI (Justice, Equity, Diversity, and Inclusion); IDEA (Inclusion, Diversity, Equity, and Accessibility); DEIA (Diversity, Equity, Inclusion, and Accessibility); and DEIJ (Diversity, Equity, Inclusion, and Justice) are just some examples that have led to confusion. As the CEO of a Diversity consulting firm lamented, "DEI has only been the acronym *du jour* since 2020. Regardless of what we call it, we've done a really poor job storytelling what this work is actually about."[3]

WHAT DEIB IS

To understand what genuine DEIB is as a societal objective, we first need to define each word that comprises the acronym.

---

[3] Taylor, Telford & Mark, Julian. "DEI is getting a new name. Can it dump the political baggage?" The Washington Post, May 5, 2024, https://www. washingtonpost.com/business/2024/05/05/dei-affirmative-action-rebrand-evolution/.

Diversity is all the ways in which individuals are unique; it is the total sum of the person. Holistically speaking, there are more than twenty-two Dimensions of Diversity. They include:

DIMENSIONS OF DIVERSITY	
Age	Lived Experience
Communication Styles	Multiculturalism
Disability / Capability / Accessibility	Race, Ethnicity, Hue of Skin
Gender, Sexual Orientation, Gender Identity, Gender Expression	Religion
Generations	Skills, Knowledge
Geography	Socioeconomics (wealth, upper income, middle class, lower income, working poor, poverty, below poverty)
Health Care Status, Sense of Wellness	Veterans

Equity is a behavioral tool.

What is Equity?

CONNECT
ENGAGE
ACHIEVE

❖ Equity is a **behavioral tool** for quickly and easily establishing a society where **all groups** are **genuinely equal.** "Equity" speaks to the **condition of a society** as a whole, **not** just individuals as compared to other individuals

Fairness Impartiality

A Belonging Enabler

Equity is often used interchangeably with equality, but they are not the same—in fact, there are significant differences.

What is Equal / Equality/?

❖ The state of being equal, especially in status, rights, and opportunities

❖ What is the best definition for Equality?

- Equality is about ensuring that **every individual** has an equal opportunity to make the most of their lives and talents.

- It is also the belief that no one should have poorer life changes because of how they were assigned at birth, where they come from, what they believe, or whether they have a disability.

- What are the three categories of Equality?
  1. Political
  2. Social
  3. Economic

Inclusion is taking everyone into account and creating an environment that encourages individuals to be themselves, however perceived to be unique, so they can thrive; and ensures everyone feels valued.

Belonging is being taken in and accepted as part of a group. A sense of Belonging occurs when a person feels that they are part of something bigger than themselves and, therefore, recognizes the rest of the members of their reference group as equals.

Collectively, DEIB is the deliberate, organized, and sustained actions necessary to: (1) educate organizations, institutions, and other entities about the many Dimensions of Diversity, which extend beyond race, ethnicity, and gender; and (2) help them identify and adopt behaviors and practices that: bring traditionally excluded individuals and groups into processes, activities, and decision/policymaking in a way that shares power and ensures equal access to opportunities and resources (Inclusion) and ensures fair treatment, access, opportunity, and advancement for all while striving to identify and eliminate barriers that have prevented the full participation of some individuals and groups (Equity), resulting in a culture of Belonging.

Clarifying DEIB

CONNECT
ENGAGE
ACHIEVE

Diversity
Equity
Inclusion
=
↓
Belonging

❖ DEIB is about Humanity: You and Me, All of Us

o All human beings possess **multiple** dimensions of diversity

o How we treat and value each other, mutual respect, fairness

o The Principle of valuing and leveraging each individual's knowledge, abilities, lived experience, and creativity (what one brings to the table)

"Out of Many, One"
"E pluribus unum"

Source: THE VEREEN GROUP
DEIB Level Set Discovery Learning

Debating the shorthand used to reference principles that touch every human being only serves to undermine the credibility of DEIB initiatives everywhere. Ongoing arguments about the "correct" branding for qualities so integral to humanity as mutual respect and the quest for equality only make progress more difficult to achieve. It is a waste of precious time and resources, and a distraction that those trying to advance DEIB can ill afford.

Does anyone really believe that those fighting DEI/DEIB will ever accept a particular acronym? Indeed, opponents of DEIB Principles are undoubtedly bemused, and perhaps relieved, by an apparent inability to embrace a mantle as forcefully as the leaders of the Civil Rights Movement did. It's time for supporters of DEIB Principles to put their pencils down. Let's spend our energy systematically implementing sustainable initiatives drawn from those Principles to strengthen organizations and, ultimately, society as a whole.

WHAT DEIB IS NOT

It's important to note here that efforts to advance DEIB Principles have also been hampered by campaigns to treat it as synonymous with, or adjacent to, what can amount to unlawful actions. In an age where so many have succumbed to illusory truth (the tendency to believe false information is correct after hearing it many times), it is necessary to set the record straight. (In Chapter 3, "Norms and Laws," we expand upon the contrast between DEIB, and the aspects of law discussed below.)

DEIB is not about race, gender, hue of skin, or socioeconomics replacement.

DEIB is not about placing blame for the past mistreatment of various groups or trying to rewrite U.S. history. Previously excluded accounts of mistreatment are part of the country's history.

DEIB Is not about "bashing" white males. They are part of our diverse population and possess their own multiple Dimensions of Diversity.

DEIB is not compliance. In 1964, Congress established the U.S. Equal Employment Opportunity Commission (**EEOC**)[4] to enforce Title VII of the Civil Rights Act of 1964. Since then, its responsibilities have grown to include the enforcement of several federal laws that make it illegal to discriminate against a job applicant or an employee because of the person's race, color, religion, sex (including pregnancy, childbirth or related conditions, transgender status, and sexual orientation), national origin, age (forty or older), disability, or **genetic information**. It also makes it illegal for an employer to retaliate against an employee for reporting discrimination or harassment.

Most employers with at least fifteen employees (twenty employees in age discrimination cases) are covered by **EEOC laws**. Most labor unions and employment agencies are also covered. The laws apply to all types of work situations, including hiring, firing, promotions, harassment, training, wages, and benefits. Workplace compliance involves adhering to relevant laws, regulations, and internal policies to ensure a safe and fair work environment, mitigating risks, and promoting ethical conduct.

While DEIB and EEO (Equal Employment Opportunity) are certainly related, they are best described as cousins, rather than siblings. DEIB is not another form of the EEOC. It is not about enforcing EEO Laws; it has a much broader scope. Many of the Dimensions of Diversity are not covered by the laws administered by the EEOC.

---

[4] EEOC.gov.

DEIB is about humanity. Moreover, while DEIB supports the enforcement of laws enacted to deter unfair treatment, its approach is one of informing, educating, and enabling systemic change. Its objective is not legal compliance; it strives to develop societal norms that result in a culture of Belonging for everyone.

DEIB

DEIB and EEO Are Cousins They ARE NOT Siblings

EEO

HUMANITY / VALUES / FORWARD THINKING / HIGH PERFORMANCE / "Out Of Many, One"
- Diversity
- Equity
- Inclusion
- Belonging
- Parity
- Dimensions of Diversity
- Inclusion Enablers
- Mission, Values Alignment
- Color Brave Society: Seen/Valued

Diversity Equity Inclusion = Belonging

LAWS/COMPLIANCE
- ✓ Civil Rights
- ✓ Equal / Equality
- ✓ Affirmative Action
- ✓ Establishing Quotas
- ✓ EEOC (Equal Employment Opportunity Commission)
- ✓ Color-Blind Society: Invisible

*Words Matter: Vision, Mission, Core Values, and Demonstrated Behaviors Reflecting Your Words **Matter Most** for a Trustworthy Brand Identity. "Walking the Talk"*

Source: THE VEREEN GROUP
DEIB Level Set Discovery Learning

DEIB is not affirmative action. Affirmative Action is the product of policies, legislation, programs, and procedures to improve the educational or employment opportunities of members of certain demographics. It originated as a public policy on March 6, 1961, when President John F. Kennedy issued Executive Order 10925. The Order included a provision that government contractors "take affirmative action to ensure that applicants are employed, and employees are treated during employment, without regard to their race, creed, color, or national origin." Since then, Affirmative Action laws and programs have been implemented to cover additional individuals and groups.

The primary purpose of Affirmative Action measures is to remedy the effects of widespread racial discrimination dating back to the earliest days of what became the United States. Some of these laws and regulations have been challenged as unconstitutional, and in 2023 the U.S. Supreme Court found that admissions practices at certain colleges and universities violated the Equal Protection Clause of the Fourteenth Amendment.[5]

DEIB does not advocate the use of race, or any other Dimension of Diversity, to define the worth of an individual. It does not support initiatives that give an individual an advantage in hiring, promotion, or similar decisions because they possess a particular Dimension (Black, female, White, disabled, et cetera), *unless* the Dimension is an objectively valid qualification (e.g., female to be a wet nurse). Such exceptions are few and far between.

DEIB practices are not focused on any single Dimension. On the contrary, they encourage an approach designed to value and leverage each individual's knowledge, abilities, lived experience, and creativity—the whole individual—to evaluate what they bring to the table.

DEIB is not reverse discrimination. When most people think of a discriminatory situation, they tend to consider actions taken against groups among the minority in the United States, that is, Persons of Color. (We do not endorse the use of the word "minorities"

---

[5] Students for Fair Admissions, Inc. v. President and Fellows of Harvard College, 600 U.S. ___ (2023).

as it implies that the people so labeled are "less than" those in the majority.) "Reverse discrimination" is said to occur when a member of the majority group—currently, Whites—is discriminated against. It is equally wrong and just as illegal as "regular" discrimination. **Unlawful discrimination** is unlawful discrimination—whether the victim of discrimination is Black or White; male or female; Christian, Jewish, Muslim, or Atheist; disabled or able-bodied. In fact, the term reverse discrimination has no legal significance whatsoever.

DEIB does not, and has never, encouraged discrimination of any kind. DEIB Principles are nondiscriminatory. In a society that fully embraces the practice of DEIB Principles, instances of unlawful discrimination would eventually become a thing of the past.

DEIB is not unconstitutional. Under our system of government, the United States Supreme Court has the sole authority to determine what laws, executive orders, regulations, and practices are unconstitutional. DEIB is none of these. It is a group of Principles that inform a belief in how humans should treat and value one another.

DEIB is not illegal. For the same reasons that DEIB has not been declared unconstitutional, it has also not been declared illegal.

DEIB is not a zero-sum proposition—or situation where someone must have less for another to have more.

DEIB is not about siloing, separating, or a stand-alone concept within an organization.

DEIB is not about you look like me, sound like me, think like me, went to the same school as me, or are a "good fit."

"Past Behavior Without Lessons Learned Will Be/Is Today's Behavior"

An Early Real-Life Lesson was to better understand the DEIB and EEOC terminology. We created an **Internal Glossary of Key Diverse Terms** to not only raise awareness and educate the organization, but to ensure less miscommunication as we all learned and grew together. The Glossary was introduced and shared across the organization, placed on organization's "SharePoint" drive with easy access for all associates, and used in professional, and career path development sessions as well. It was continually updated as the language evolved. The organization came to love the communication and engagement doors it opened.

"One of the Best Tools ever;
and we're sharing with You!"

CHAPTER 3

NORMS AND LAWS

The relationship between a society's **norms** and laws is central to understanding DEIB and being able to effectively advocate its Principles. To help evolve the norms of an organization, one first must discern how they came to be.

As discussed in Chapter 1, DEIB is viewed by many as a proxy for practices prohibited by law or for policies with which they disagree, such as Affirmative Action or "reverse discrimination." Additional misunderstandings stem from the impression that laws have an impact merely by virtue of being enacted. Yes, laws mandate ("shall") or prohibit ("shall not") certain actions, but the groups and individuals that **civil rights laws** are meant to protect were not, and are not, treated fairly throughout society merely because some laws have been enacted or changed. For this to happen, societal norms must adjust as well.

Another erroneous belief—that laws and norms are the same thing—has also frustrated efforts to weave DEIB Principles into how an organization operates. Societal norms are shared expectations within a given society about how members should behave and interact with one another. They are often informal and unwritten. While some U.S. laws reflect norms (for example, laws prohibiting theft), and in some instances influence changes to norms (such as laws outlawing child labor), they do not address all the ways in which our society functions. There is no legal requirement to hold a door open for an individual carrying a child, for instance, but this occurs regularly throughout the country.

While DEIB supports the enforcement of laws enacted to deter unfair treatment, its objective goes far beyond legal compliance. DEIB is about humanity, how we value and treat each other. Thus, it strives to develop societal norms that result in a Culture of Belonging for everyone. DEIB's approach is one of informing, educating, and helping others adopt behaviors and practices that result in such a culture. Only then will the United States be able to deliver on its promise of equality for all.

Martin Luther King Jr. once observed, "We are not makers of history. We are made by history."[6] While no two members of society share identical experiences, we are all subject to societal norms—as well as laws and their application—that evolved as society was impacted by, and responded to, the events that have occurred over its existence. The treatment of members of U.S. society possessing certain Dimensions of Diversity can best be understood by examining this evolution—our history.

---

[6] King, Martin Luther Jr. "Transformed Nonconformist." Delivered at Dexter Avenue Baptist Church, Montgomery, Alabama, 1954.

All organizations exist within a larger and diverse society and are comprised of its members. For this reason, we advise "meeting an organization where it is" on the DEIB Journey. To do that, a DEIB Leader needs to understand what the organization's norms are and why they prevail. This necessarily includes an understanding of societal history, both past and as it is being created.

An incomplete or inaccurate historical perspective about DEIB held by individuals within an organization is often a major barrier to progress. This barrier can only be broken down through education by someone with adequate knowledge of, and the ability to explain, history within the context of DEIB Principles.

An assessment of the relationship between U.S. society's norms and its laws requires fundamental knowledge of three areas: (1) the elements of the U.S. system of government, sometimes referred to as "Civics"; (2) the definition and purpose of laws; and (3) U.S. history, particularly as it pertains to the treatment of people.

Hopefully, you already understand the mechanics of how a particular piece of legislation becomes law. You also recognize that the judges who interpret those laws possess different perspectives from the ones they succeeded and/or those who follow them. Similarly, you can appreciate why two states can adopt laws that seem to be at odds with one another. In short, you have a basic understanding of how the U.S. system of government is structured, as well as how it has evolved over time.

It is noteworthy, though, that a significant portion of the public doesn't know or understand the fundamentals of American government. A 2021 Annenberg Constitution Day Civics Survey found that more than four out of ten of our adult fellow citizens (44 percent) could not identify the three branches of the U.S. government.[7] One-fifth could not name any.

Rather than assume that readers are well-versed in these areas, we provide a very brief exposition on each. If it is too rudimentary for you, we apologize. Feel free to skip straight to the section "Civil Rights Laws and Norms," which follows our short civics lesson.

SYSTEM OF GOVERNMENT

The United States is made up of fifty states and the District of Columbia. Several territories are controlled by the U.S. (Puerto Rico, Guam, and American Samoa, to name some), but they do not have the same rights as the states. Most states and territories are comprised of smaller governmental units based on geography, such as counties, cities, and other municipalities (e.g., towns, boroughs, and villages).

FEDERAL

STATE

| COUNTY | CITY | MUNICPALITY |

---

[7] "Americans' Civic Knowledge Increases During a Stress-filled Year." Annenberg Public Policy Center. University of Pennsylvania. Sept. 14, 2021. https://www.annenbergpublicpolicycenter.org/2021-annenberg-constitution-day-civics-survey/.

ORGANIZATION

The federal government of the United States consists of three branches: (1) the legislature, (2) the executive, and (3) the judiciary. Each state and the District of Columbia also governs utilizing a chief executive (usually, a governor), legislature, and judiciary.

Legislature	Executive	Judiciary
House of Representatives Senate	President Cabinet Officers Departments	Supreme Court Appeals Courts District Courts

The federal *legislative branch* is comprised of the two houses of Congress: the Senate and the House of Representatives. The most important duty of the legislative branch is to make laws. Laws are written, discussed, and voted on in Congress. There are one hundred senators in the Senate, two from each state. Senators are elected by their states and serve six-year terms. There are 435 representatives in the House of Representatives. The number of representatives allotted to each state is based on its population. Representatives are elected by their districts and serve two-year terms.

The *executive branch* is headed by the President of the United States, who is elected by the entire country, serves a four-year term, and potentially can be elected for a second term. The President approves or vetoes legislation passed by the legislative branch and appoints or removes cabinet members (Secretary of State, Attorney General, as well as the other heads of the Executive Departments) and officials.

The *judicial branch* oversees the court system of the U.S. and, through court cases, interprets the meaning of the Constitution and laws passed by Congress. The Supreme Court is the head of the judicial branch and is comprised of nine justices—eight associate justices and one chief justice. There are ninety-four District Courts, where trials are held. Federal appeals courts, of which there are thirteen, hear appeals from district courts.

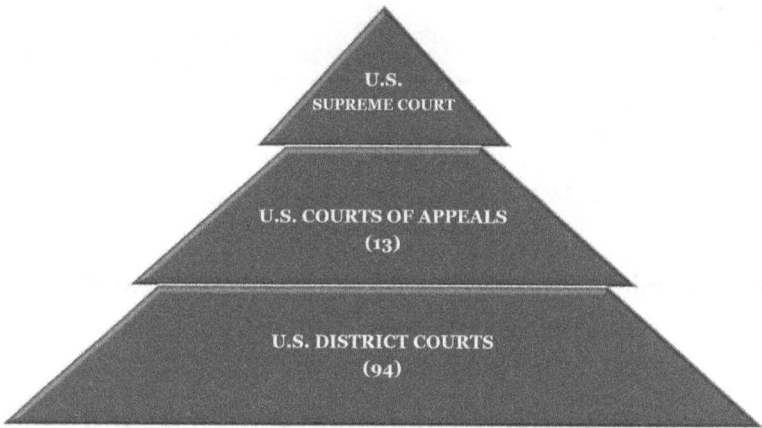

Supreme Court justices, and other federal judges that fall under Article III of the Constitution, are nominated by the President and approved by the Senate. They have no term limits.

Recognizing that it is impossible to anticipate every circumstance society may encounter, laws and regulations enacted by governing bodies at the federal, state, and local levels are subject to interpretation. When there is a dispute over what the words mean, it is often the judicial branch of government that provides the interpretation. In fact, these laws and regulations are often expressly designed to include language establishing certain standards, which then are applied to a specific set of facts and interpreted at a particular point in time. What that standard means and how it is applied can change as society's norms change.

Laws

"Law" has been defined as "a body of rules of action or conduct prescribed by a controlling authority and having binding legal force. That which must be obeyed and followed by citizens subject to sanctions or legal consequences is a law."[8] Laws mandate ("shall") or prohibit ("shall not") certain actions. They are created by the legislature, interpreted by the courts, and enforced by agencies within the executive branch, such as the FBI and, at the state and local level, by agencies such as police forces.

The purpose of laws is to bring order to a society. In the United States, laws also establish certain standards, protect rights, and provide a framework for resolving disputes.

The sheer breadth of providing order to society prohibits, as a practical matter, the direct input of all citizens into every decision required to govern. So it is that all individuals and organizations are subject to laws that apply to our entire country, as well as those of the state, territory, county, municipality, township, or other governmental subset in which they live. Why and how those laws are created and enforced is of great consequence to DEIB initiatives.

Only the legislative branch of the federal and state government has the power to make laws. If enough members of each part of the legislature (House and Senate) approve a law, it must then be signed by the chief executive (the President or a governor) to become a law.

While the judicial branch does not make laws, the decisions of judges amount to legal authority where the court has jurisdiction, but not

---

[8] Law. Black's Law Dictionary. (Sixth ed. 1990).

elsewhere. For example, a decision by a state judge in Pennsylvania is not binding legal authority for people living outside of Pennsylvania. Similarly, a decision by the federal appellate court that covers Texas, Louisiana, and Mississippi (The Fifth Circuit Court of Appeals) does not have to be followed by citizens living outside of those states. When there are conflicting decisions about significant legal issues among the federal courts of appeals, it is up to the U.S. Supreme Court to resolve them by issuing its own ruling, which cannot be appealed.

The executive branch does not have the authority to make laws. The President or a state governor may issue Executive Orders to those individuals and departments which are part of the executive branch to provide direction on how to implement a law, but they cannot change an existing law or create a new one. Only the legislature can do that.[9]

History

What, you may well ask, does history have to do with DEIB? Is not the entire point of DEIB to look forward, not backward, to create a more inclusive society than currently exists? These are fair questions that demand answers, especially for those who have grown increasingly impatient with the pace at which U.S. society has moved toward achieving equality.

A DEIB Leader's objective is to help their organization evolve toward a sustainable Culture of Belonging. Recall that all organizations exist within the larger society; moreover, the organizations'

---

[9] Additional information can be found in the American Bar Association's "What Is An Executive Order?" https://www.americanbar.org/groups/public_education/publications/teaching-legal-docs/what-is-an-executive-order-/.

members bring with them their own experiences and perspectives, which are largely influenced by that society and its history. An incomplete or inaccurate historical perspective about DEIB held by individuals within an organization is often a major challenge to progress. This challenge can only be addressed through education by someone with adequate knowledge of, and the ability to bring clarity about, history within the context of DEIB Principles.

History is not merely a chronological listing of influential writings or well-known events. Rather, it is a portrayal of how society functioned at any point along its existence and why its norms changed or didn't.

Learning history means gaining some skill in sorting through diverse, often conflicting interpretations. Understanding how societies work—the central goal of historical study—is inherently imprecise, and the same certainly holds true for understanding what is going on in the present day. Learning how to identify and evaluate conflicting interpretations is an essential citizenship skill for which history, as an often-contested laboratory of human experience, provides training. This is one area in which the full benefits of historical study sometimes clash with the narrower uses of the past to construct identity. Experience in examining past situations provides a constructively critical sense that can be applied to partisan claims about the glories of national or group identity. The study of history in no sense undermines loyalty or commitment, but it does teach the need for assessing arguments, and it provides opportunities to engage in debate and achieve perspective.[10]

---

[10] Stearns, Peter N. "History of the Discipline, Teaching Methods." n.d. https://www.historians.org/resource/why-study-history-1998/.

Recall that DEIB includes the deliberate, organized, and sustained actions necessary to educate organizations about the many Dimensions of Diversity, and help them identify and adopt behaviors and practices that bring *traditionally excluded individuals and groups* into processes, activities, and decision/policymaking in a way that shares value and power and ensures equal access to opportunities and resources (Inclusion).

"What's past is prologue." This phase, which is engraved on the National Archives Building in Washington, DC, stands for the idea that history sets the context for the present. An important benefit of knowing history is that it develops an ability to anticipate trends before they happen.

Another saying, "History repeats itself and sometimes rhymes," is also rightly accepted as true. An understanding of the patterns of history gives the DEIB Leader the awareness that we have been here before—and the lessons learned—that informs decisions based on critical thinking. While this work is indeed future-oriented, the future unfolds from the past.

Tradition is the transmission of customs, practices, and beliefs from one generation to another. Thus, one can only gain a working knowledge of which individuals and groups have been "traditionally excluded," by whom they were excluded, and from what they were excluded, through an understanding of history.

The perception of history held by those with authority plays a significant role in its attitudes about what should and should not be part of society's norms. Indeed, those individuals with the power to help an organization evolve have a **World View** that has been shaped from *their perspective* of history—one which is not necessarily complete or accurate. Regardless, it is where they are.

Often, the descriptions of history to which they have been exposed are incomplete or biased, be it consciously or unconsciously. To break down resistance to DEIB initiatives that may arise from these misperceptions, a DEIB Leader must be equipped to convincingly set the record straight and realign perceptions with a World View that takes into account aspects that were heretofore ignored or discounted.

This is not a history book. An attempt here to summarize U.S. history as it relates to DEIB would be woefully incomplete. What we can do is highlight the import of history and provide examples of the need to look beyond a historical event to the impact that flowed from it.

CIVIL RIGHTS LAWS AND NORMS

President John Adams, who signed the Declaration of Independence, observed that "ours is a government of laws, not of men."[11] The pronouncement is aspirational; the real impact on government and U.S. society from the passage of a new law is commonly misunderstood.

The import of the collection of words drafted by a legislature, then signed into law by the President or state governor, cannot be fully appreciated until well after the law becomes effective. It is not until those words are interpreted by the appropriate authorities, and rules contained in those words are enforced, that the law's actual effect on society becomes known.

---

[11] "III. Thoughts on Government, April 1776," *Founders Online*, National Archives, https://founders.archives.gov/documents/Adams/06-04-02-0026-0004. [Original source: *The Adams Papers*, Papers of John Adams, vol. 4, *February–August 1776*, ed. Robert J. Taylor. Cambridge, MA: Harvard University Press, 1979, pp. 86–93.]

Laws themselves, including the mandates and proscriptions of the U.S. Constitution itself, are not self-enforcing. That is, the mere act of a government adopting a law does not in and of itself serve to bring about the results the law is meant to achieve. Simply approving language that makes it a crime to steal does not prevent stealing. Prohibiting discrimination based on a person's race did not end the practice. How the law is enforced and the penalties associated with violations are applied have much to do with the extent to which it influences the behavior of society—its norms.

Stated more succinctly: Legal rights are *not* the equivalent of societal norms for exercising those rights. The members of society with the authority or power to interpret and enforce laws define the scope of the rights, which becomes the prevailing norm. This has been true throughout U.S. history and continues today.

Some believe that everyone has always been equal in the United States, based on the fact that the Declaration of Independence states that "all men are created equal." Those words do, in fact, appear in the Declaration. The complete quote is, "We hold these truths to be self-evident, that all men are created equal, that they are endowed by their Creator with certain unalienable Rights, that among these are Life, Liberty and the pursuit of Happiness."

Taken at face value, it does appear that the Founders believed in equality for all (assuming "men" was used to denote the broader "mankind," not a specific gender). But history informs us that this was not the case. How do we know that? By examining how those words were interpreted by those with the authority and power to do so. Words have little or no effect until they are acted upon; hence, "Actions speak louder than words." The interpretation of our governing documents and laws, as demonstrated by subsequent actions, gives life to history.

The Declaration of Independence did, indeed, describe the unalienable rights of men—White men. The enslavement of Persons of Color, codified eleven years later in Article 1 of the U.S. Constitution, in which each enslaved person counted only as three-fifths of a human being for purposes of determining the population of a state[12] and the denial of voting rights to women until 1920, are but two examples.

When called upon to interpret the language of the Constitution, the United States Supreme Court has validated discrimination against Persons of Color for the majority of the country's history. In 1857, eighty-one years after the Founders declared that all men are created equal, the Court ruled that Congress could not limit slavery and that Americans of African descent had no right to sue. Even after the Civil War and the passage of the 13th Amendment, which abolished slavery, the Supreme Court in 1896 found that the Constitution allowed for **segregation** based on the hue of a person's skin. This was 120 years after declaring all men to be equal, and twenty-eight years after the Equal Protection Clause of the 14th Amendment became law.

From the time Europeans began to colonize what we now call the United States until the mid-twentieth century, the country's laws and norms accorded Persons of Color a status that was less than and subservient to White citizens. Change in the law finally came in 1954, when the Supreme Court ruled in *Brown v. Board of Education*[13] that the "separate but equal" doctrine was unconstitutional. This was 335 years after the first of the enslaved Africans were brought to Virginia Colony, and 178 years since the colonies declared their intent to form a new nation.

---

[12] Each state is allotted a proportional number of members of the House of Representatives based upon population. No right to vote accompanied their Inclusion in the Constitution; the enslaved were treated as nothing more than a statistic.

[13] *Brown v. Board of Education*, 347 U.S. 483 (1954).

Why did the Court change course from its 1896 decision? Because some racial norms had begun to evolve. Moreover, the Justices on the Supreme Court in 1954 were different from those who decided the 1896 case.

Did this mean that, beginning immediately after the Supreme Court issued its decision to prohibit segregation, officials and businesses across the country took steps to end exclusion and integrate all races? No, not at all. As the Supreme Court Justices and other members of the judiciary do not enforce the laws, it was left to others in power to further interpret and enforce the Court's decision.

Many state and local governments resisted integration, choosing instead to interpret the <u>Brown</u> decision narrowly. Those opposed to integration argued that requiring Persons of Color to sit at the back of a bus did not constitute "separate but equal" treatment. Rather, they suggested, it was equal treatment for everyone, Black and White. Both groups rode the same bus, which stopped at the same destinations for all passengers. In this instance, authority delivered its interpretation of the law.

The right to vote is another stark example of the frequent inconsistency of a society's laws and norms. Long after the ratification of the 15th Amendment in 1870, prohibiting the denial of the right to vote based upon "race, color, or previous condition of servitude," a former slave brave enough to try to register to vote was almost certain to be met with refusal, if not worse treatment. Women would have to wait another fifty years (1920) until the 19th Amendment was added to the Constitution, finally "granting" them the right to vote.

Poll taxes and literacy tests were employed by many states to prevent African Americans from voting; several made it a crime to teach an enslaved person how to read. Until 1915, when the U.S. Supreme Court found the practice to be unconstitutional, a number of states employed a "grandfather clause" to prevent descendants of the enslaved from voting. African American men, almost all of whom were descendants of ancestors who had been enslaved, were prohibited from voting unless they could prove that their grandfather had voted.

Nearly 100 years later, in 1965, the Voting Rights Act was passed as a further effort to clear the way for the formerly enslaved and their descendants to vote—an effort that continues to this day.

It was only because people in real situations continued to challenge authority/power that the contours of the Supreme Court's decision began to take shape. For example, requiring a non-White to sit at the back of a public bus was found to be unlawful segregation only because in 1955 Rosa Parks refused to move, resulting in her arrest. Her subsequent challenge to these actions eventually found its way to the Supreme Court. In late 1956, the Court ruled that such bus segregation was unconstitutional.

These are only a few illustrations that society is not a reflection of its laws, but of its *actions* under those laws. A firm grasp of this concept is crucial to being an effective DEIB Leader.

To sum up, those unreceptive to evolving for the purpose of improving DEIB practices often latch onto the fact that a certain law or laws exist. This, they contend, establishes equality; nothing more need be done. In order to meet someone at their current level of understanding of DEIB, a DEIB Leader must be able to explain the relationship between norms and its laws, particularly Civil Rights laws, and how adopting DEIB Principles and practices helps society live up to the intent of those laws.

PART 2

SYSTEMIC CHANGE

CHAPTER 4

WHY MOST DEIB INITIATIVES HAVE FAILED

While many organizations have made sincere efforts and invested significant resources to bring Diversity, Equity, Inclusion, and Belonging into their workplaces, few, if any, have succeeded in making DEIB Principles and practices part of their **DNA**. In their haste to demonstrate a commitment to Diversity, most organizations neglect to educate themselves about the breadth of DEIB and its impact upon the workplace, and society in general, forging ahead without a cohesive, holistic plan. The result is that their DEIB initiatives don't have a long-term impact on organizational culture or create systemic change.

For more than two decades, we have worked as employees of and outside advisors to organizations and DEIB professionals, interacting with hundreds of individuals who work in the DEIB Discipline or are committed supporters of its Principles. We have regularly engaged with board members, executives, managers, and Human Resources staff about DEIB at their organization. Through our experience, we've identified the common cause that explains why most DEIB initiatives don't translate into sustainable systemic change: the failure of organizations to empower, with sustainable support, qualified internal DEIB Leaders in the systematic implementation journey of a strategic, holistic (enterprise-wide) framework.

To be sure, DEIB faces many inherent challenges. Talk with any number of DEIB Leaders and you'll hear recurring themes about what they find to be the most daunting aspect of advancing initiatives.

We must point out that those focused upon bringing about change of any kind face an uphill battle. Generally speaking, human beings don't like change. We are comfortable in our known environment. Altering that environment can be quite frightening, especially given the uncertainty of what our experience will be after change has taken place.

Being is also easier than becoming. We already know how to do the things we do routinely; change requires us to learn and practice new behaviors. Take dieting, for instance. Whatever our health objectives—losing weight, reducing cholesterol, lowering blood pressure—we need to change how we eat. To do that, we must practice new behaviors that involve food selection and consumption.

The same holds for how we treat other people. If one is used to treating members of a certain group as inferior, they need to modify their behavior to be consistent with the definition and Principles of DEIB (as covered in Chapter 2).

As change tends to be resisted, and considering that the very mission of DEIB work, its *raison d'être*, is to enhance an organization's environment, it's no wonder that when modifications do take place, they often come at a very slow pace. Those comfortable with the *status quo* are in no rush, while those committed to DEIB Principles, who understand that the rights and treatment of human beings are at stake, see an urgency.

Perhaps related to the general resistance to change, some organizations simply don't perceive a need for DEIB and aren't convinced that it brings any benefits. They haven't thought about the role of DEIB at their organization in a meaningful way. They've not considered how it adds value.

Even entities that have designated positions or departments to address DEIB (Diversity Director, Chief Equity Officer, Office of Inclusion, and the like) may not actually believe there are any issues that warrant significant modifications to their work environment and practices. Maybe they've included DEIB as part of the organizational chart because that's what everyone else is doing, but they don't see a real need for it. As far as they're concerned, existing laws and policies are "good enough."

For some, the election of a Black President and, subsequently, Vice President of Color, is proof that equality already exists. They are puzzled by notions of systemic racism and discrimination when the highest offices in the land have been held by Persons of Color.

DEIB is also viewed by some as a legal issue that is already being addressed. Non-discrimination laws (EEO) have worked, they believe, and as their organization is subject to the same laws, the proper framework is already in place.

Existing non-discrimination laws and Affirmative Action programs are considered to be DEIB policies that have been forced upon employers by the government. DEIB may come to be seen as another form of unsolicited interference. Keep in mind, as explained in Chapter 2, DEIB *is not* the same as EEO.

Other organizations recognize that inequities exist "out there" (in establishments other than their own). They profess not to see color (Color Blind Society) and are convinced that all their decisions are based purely on individual merit. They may be willing to go along with certain aspects of DEIB, such as "awareness" sessions and training, but they stop far short of significant process and procedure changes in areas like marketing, communications, advertising, services, products, hiring, retention, promotion, succession planning, and compensation—in other words, practices that cut across and define the entire organization.

Unfortunately, DEIB can be seen, inaccurately, as a burden, adding yet another responsibility to an already extensive list of managerial duties. This is unfamiliar territory, so they are quick to look for someone else to address it, leading to a lack of guidance for those ultimately charged with creating and implementing DEIB practices across the organization.

Another factor is the organization's current financial position. Interestingly, while many change strategists advise that it is best to make significant modifications when an organization is in a position of strength, managers commonly take the opposite stance—also known as, "If it isn't broken don't fix it." They fear that change, including DEIB, will have a negative effect, when the opposite is true.

Some organizations, including those who genuinely want to make DEIB Principles part of who they are, simply don't believe it fits within the existing structure. Accounting. Operations. Legal. Marketing. Finance, Sales. Human Resources. Facilities Departments. Divisions.

Revenue. Expenses. These and other components are part of how nearly every organization functions, be it a nonprofit or for-profit enterprise, and have been since each was formed. Leadership has experience working with most, if not all, of these areas.

The same cannot be said of DEIB, which is relatively new— not conceptually, but as something organizations have considered integrating into their operating structure. A DEIB-related position or department is still not universally part of every organization. Organizations have little, if any, experience with how DEIB exists within any structure, and are not sure what to make of it. Rarely, too, does an organization's senior leadership include a DEIB Professional among its members. As a result, the former often doesn't know how to effectively manage and work with the latter.

This situation is exacerbated by the difficulty of measuring the impact of DEIB-related initiatives. Revered management consultant Peter Drucker championed the notion that if something can't be measured, it can't be managed. Revenue goes up or down, measured in dollars and percentages. The same is true of expenses and sales. Even marketing has developed analytics that statistic-hungry managers can understand. Targets linked to compensation can be developed with a fair level of clarity of the objectives and how success is to be measured.

This philosophy pervades the world of business, and the nonprofit sector is not immune to its appeal either. Newsletters and annual reports feature pie charts, bar graphs, and all manner of statistics to show how donors' money is being used to carry out the organization's mission.

Recognizing the need to provide metrics, the DEIB Discipline has developed some measurement tools. Employee satisfaction surveys and stock performance ranking based upon the strength of each company's DEIB programs are but two examples. Nevertheless, leadership generally views these "statistics" with skepticism, owing to the inherent subjectivity in measuring concepts like inclusiveness and equity. Diversity, while somewhat easier to measure if limited to the most readily identifiable groups, such as Whites/non-Whites or female/male, is also much more complex than a simple, two-category representation of race and gender headcount.

Couple the difficulty of measuring how an organization is doing on the DEIB scale with the challenge of even agreeing on what DEIB success looks like, and it is small wonder that many organizations fail to see DEIB as a priority. They may quickly come to view it as a "soft" part of management or, worse, a necessary evil that has been foisted upon them, adding to their already heavy workload.

Whatever the reason, organizations rarely view DEIB as a priority for success. As too many Diversity Directors have experienced, when the organization is asked to cut back on expenses, DEIB funding is usually one of the first victims.

Contributing to the difficulty of adding DEIB to an organization's structure is the fact that no generally recognized model exists. Other disciplines have well-established rules, regulations, and best practices upon which an organization's management can rely to be assured that the organization is operating within industry norms.

For example, accounting and finance functions are subject to review under the Generally Accepted Accounting Principles that began to be created in the mid-1930s as the result of the passage of the Securities Exchange Act. Boards of Directors and their advisors also can look to several public sources for guidance on how to carry out their duties, including the Sarbanes-Oxley Act of 2002.

Risk management, cybersecurity, safety, employee relations, and legal departments have a plethora of resources and standards to help them properly carry out their duties. These also allow them to show their bosses that they are operating in the mainstream with time-tested procedures and practices. At a minimum, they provide management and the board of directors with something of an insurance policy (posterior coverage!) if something goes awry.

Not so with DEIB. While the DEIB discipline now includes any number of associations, publications, and tools—owing to the fact that DEIB involves every aspect of an organization where humans are present—it does not lend itself to impartial objectivity. A standard approach to creating an optimal DEIB environment that can be replicated at any given organization is unlikely to ever be created. There are too many variables: the composition of the organization, where it is on the DEIB journey, location(s), size, customer base—the list goes on.

An online search of "Diversity best practices" yields millions of different results. There are thousands of books covering DEIB topics. Even the "best" DEIB books, however, leave one quickly overwhelmed with differing approaches and no authoritative treatment of the subject or, more importantly, the "how to" guidance so many supporters of DEIB Principles seek.

As discussed in Chapter 3, "Norms and Laws," there are plenty of laws, rules, and regulations related to the treatment of humans based upon a range of individual or group characteristics. These directives, however, are defensive by nature, specifically describing what an organization must *not* do lest it suffer financial or other penalties. While certainly a key component in creating a legal framework to mitigate the perpetuation of past discriminatory practices, these measures alone are anything but a guide for achieving DEIB objectives and most definitely do not lead to greater Diversity, or to an inclusive or more equitable society.

Left unaddressed, any one of these challenges can undermine the success of DEIB initiatives. Rather than meeting them head-on, organizations that are not knowledgeable about DEIB and/or are resistant to change either ignore them or, worse, succumb to the temptation to use these challenges as reason to complain or make excuses for a lack of progress.

This negative trend will continue until a new way of thinking about DEIB is embraced. An organization's approach to DEIB must be holistic; every aspect needs to be viewed broadly and strategically, considering the current and future impact on the entire organization. DEIB must also be understood and practiced across the entire organization, in much the same way as practices like safety and ethics. It must reflect **Organizational Intelligence**, aligning to what is important to the organization-its vision, mission, core values, strategic objectives. And it must be carefully *sequenced* and thoughtfully woven into the fabric of the organization to ensure sustainable **systemic change**.

Proceeding without a coherent framework, including a communication plan that the whole organization understands, not only undermines the effectiveness of the organization's DEIB efforts but can damage its brand identity as well. When an organization is seen as emphasizing short-term actions, not genuine long-term improvement, employees and other stakeholders question the organization's sincerity, dismissing shallow one-offs as "performative DEIB."

Similarly, if DEIB initiatives are introduced prematurely, before the organization is ready, they won't last and may even weaken other DEIB efforts. And if initiatives are not sustainable, they eventually fall by the wayside.

Cultural evolution is nothing new. Many businesses have, for example, sought to integrate a genuine culture of safety or customer service into how they operate. When an organization decides to adopt specific attributes as part of its overall values and culture, it recognizes that this takes planning, and that change does not happen overnight. The same is true of embracing and leveraging DEIB.

CHAPTER 5

ALIGNING WITH WHAT IS IMPORTANT TO THE ORGANIZATION

As we've noted, most organizations that profess a commitment to DEIB lack a plan for achieving it. If they do have a framework, it is neither organic nor cohesive. DEIB is not treated as integral to the organization, but separate, with its own department and plans. Recall that *the failure to align DEIB practices with the organization's objectives is the single greatest reason why DEIB initiatives flounder, never reaching their real potential.*

Successful DEIB Leaders know where the organization is and how they are accustomed to doing things. They also recognize that its World View probably includes definitions of success without regard to Principles of DEIB. But they are prepared to make the case for evolving that World View.

The first step in creating an effective DEIB **Strategic Visioning Framework** is to identify the organization's vision, mission, values, and *existing* strategic objectives. The DEIB Leader is able to demonstrate to the organization how *its own words and aspirations* demand that DEIB practices be embraced and implemented. The DEIB Leader is adept at viewing the organization through the **DEIB Lens** and, more critically, teaching other members of the organization how to see through that lens too.

The following diagram depicts the components of a typical strategic plan for an organization, along with their relationship to one another.

VISION
(aspirational)

MISSION/PURPOSE
(inspirational)

OBJECTIVES
(achievements during specified timeframe)

STRATEGIES
(plans of action)

TACTICS
(action steps)

Organizational Strategic Plan Flow

An organization *does not* need to develop a separate DEIB mission, vision, core values, or the like, nor should it. DEIB initiatives are much better received if they are presented within a context that reveals an appreciation of the organization's purpose and operating realities. Sound ideas can be unfairly criticized or ignored altogether because they fail to take into account an important aspect of the organization's brand or operations.

As explained in greater detail in Chapter 9, Organizational Intelligence is an essential skill of a DEIB Leader. It is a predicate for evolving an organization so that it *chooses* to integrate DEIB practices into its operation, not because it was forced to. This is accomplished using the organization's own language, exploring and expanding its perceptions so it may understand how its own words encompass key DEIB concepts.

DEIB AND THE ORGANIZATION'S "CONSTITUTION"

The process of identifying an organization's DEIB objectives and end in mind starts with the words the organization uses to define itself internally and to others. How does the organization want to be seen? How does it present itself to its employees, customers, and the community? These aspirational statements take the form of vision or mission statements, core values, and public pronouncements of the organization's purpose, culture, and objectives that reveal what is important to it.

Selection of its DEIB objectives is also informed by the organization's strategic or business plan. It may be formal. It may be piecemeal. It may only be concepts shared by a few senior managers, but every organization needs a plan to operate. A DEIB Leader must have access to that plan to design DEIB initiatives to support it.

Though an organization may not always utilize DEIB terminology such as "respect" and "Inclusion" in its constitution and other self-defining materials, DEIB is intrinsic to its very existence. It must be, because *all* organizations are comprised of and serve people. It falls to the DEIB Leader to translate the organization's own language into DEIB-related concepts. Remember, an organization can only fully reach its objectives when it uses a DEIB lens to give life to its aspirations. An illustration may be useful.

FamilyMeals, Inc. is a fictional regional restaurant chain that describes itself as "a family business that serves families." Founded in 1957, its marketing materials portray what it sees as the "traditional" families of that era. Sales are in decline, and its efforts to expand by entering new markets have failed to meet expectations.

A DEIB Leader recognizes that if FamilyMeals wants to keep its "family" tagline, it needs to see its markets through a DEIB lens to understand that the families of today and tomorrow do not look like the 1950s ads and images they are displaying. After the company updates its marketing message to be more inclusive, portraying the diversity of families found throughout its region, sales steadily increase.

FamilyMeals' management was receptive to modifications to its messaging because it felt like it was able to remain true to its brand of serving families. Moreover, the chain was experiencing a decline; thus, they were not in the "if it's not broke, don't fix it" mentality that often presents a challenge to DEIB Leaders. Indeed, its bottom line improved as a result of the shift in perception of what "family" means in today's evolving generational world.

In some instances, the connection between the organization's existing self-portrait and DEIB is obvious. The organization may have a separate Diversity statement and core values around Diversity and Inclusion that provide insight into what it *thinks* it understands about DEIB. While this is useful in assessing the organization's perceptions, we again caution against establishing separate DEIB position statements. Instead, create initiatives that align with and support the organization overall.

When an organization does include DEIB language in its constitution or business plan, and/or has created an internal DEIB position declaring that DEIB is important, management has given permission to drive DEIB Principles throughout the organization. Even without using express DEIB language, those Principles are inevitably linked to the organization's purpose and plans. The DEIB Leader is ready to connect the dots. A company that declares, "We hire only the best," for example, can be shown that "the best" individuals are found across the many Dimensions of Diversity.

CONNECT THE DEIB DOTS

Crafting and executing an organization's DEIB initiatives begins with an analysis of its constitution's relationship to DEIB. This is the foundation of a DEIB Leader's Organizational Intelligence. It provides the authority to lead the organization and hold it accountable to its own stated aspirations and objectives, as opposed to being forced to change.

After identifying what is important to the organization, it is up to the DEIB Leader to connect the dots so that management (and, ultimately, the rest of the organization) understands why uniting DEIB Principles with organizational strategic objectives is the lynchpin to sustained success. *It is absolutely essential to explain how each DEIB initiative is linked to the organization's own declarations of what is important.*

"Remembering These Purposeful Aligning Components"

An Unlearn and Relearn Anew Lesson for a **Change Maker** is to always answer "The Why" and "What's In It For Me" for human beings.

Keep in mind:

The world continues to evolve as should our systems, business and workforce approaches to catch up and then be able to be an industry leader.

DEIB was not part of the "previous" U.S. organizational structure or process systems. It must be woven into the fabric of your organization, not siloed or treated as a set aside department.

There are two levels of DEIB commitment: # 1. Verbal #2. Demonstrated Behaviors. Identify where your organization is prior to starting your strategic plan. (See Chapter 6)

Your role as a DEIB Leader is to be the "informed clarity leader" and facilitate clear communication within your organization.

Do not lose sight of your End In Mind—Establish an Environment that is receptive to Inclusion which fosters an authentic Culture of Belonging.

"A Holistic Leader recognizes and addresses the interconnectedness of the individuals, teams, and the broader environment to foster sustainable success."

CHAPTER 6

MEETING AN ORGANIZATION WHERE IT IS

"It's the twenty-first century! I shouldn't have to explain why *they* created the position of DEIB Director." "*They* need to own DEIB and educate themselves." "I'm exhausted trying to make *them* see the value of DEIB." These are just some of the comments we hear from frustrated DEIB professionals—and with good reason.

Addressing the inequities in U.S. society resulting from a history of systemically enforced discrimination and separation is not the sole responsibility of DEIB professionals. It is the responsibility of all U.S. citizens.

But the fact remains that America's aspirational promise of equality, liberty, and justice for all has yet to be realized. Organizations have long had the opportunity to create an environment of Belonging, but few have done so. It is folly to expect that they will now evolve on their own merely because they should. Being right about the value of DEIB does not by itself result in change.

An organization must understand *why* policy modifications or initiatives are being implemented—in other words, how they connect to its value systems, behaviors, and practices. Change without understanding is unsustainable. Following specific mandates is isolated change, not systemic; it does not translate into evolving an organization's culture toward one of Belonging. First the why, then the how.

UNDERSTANDING THE ORGANIZATION'S LEVEL OF RECEPTIVENESS IS THE FOUNDATION FOR DEIB SYSTEMIC CHANGE

One cannot and should not force an organization to evolve without its active participation. Therefore, a DEIB Leader seeks first to understand an organization's current receptiveness before identifying the best solutions for evolving the organization's DEIB practices, environment, and culture. That insight is what allows them to bring the organization along a path that fosters receptiveness and encourages its members to ask clarifying questions, digest new information, and understand their collaborative role and **workplace expectations**.

The DEIB Leader must also determine the organization's existing level of commitment to Diversity, Equity, Inclusion, and Belonging. Is it "verbal" only, or is it "verbal *plus* demonstrated behaviors?" The answer assists in understanding the current leadership's messaging and what has or has not previously been done within the Dimensions of Diversity. This knowledge allows the DEIB Leader to think about the organization's culture and communication style, thus determining the correct collaborative approach moving forward.

Learning about the unique history of the organization is also critical for the DEIB Leader. How and why an organization has reached a particular place on the DEIB Journey reveals much about its embrace of inclusiveness, or lack thereof, as demonstrated by its policies, practices, and behaviors.

This approach to leadership is not exclusive to DEIB. "Seek first to understand, then to be understood" is one of the *7 Habits of Highly Effective People*, which is widely regarded as one of the most important leadership books ever written.[14] For DEIB Leaders, it is a must-read. By appreciating the perspective of the organization's decision-makers and influencers, a DEIB Leader can devise the best solutions for evolving its DEIB practices to ensure an inclusive environment that enables consistent progress.

A key to successfully implementing the DEIB Strategic Visioning Framework is to translate each aspect of the Framework into concepts the organization can understand. For example, the DEIB Leader must master and utilize the language of the sector they are working with (community, business, education, government). In this way, the Framework is carefully tailored so the organization can chart its unique path toward a Culture of Belonging.

DETERMINING WHERE AN ORGANIZATION IS ON ITS DEIB JOURNEY

DEIB touches every aspect of an organization; therefore, determining where it is on the DEIB Journey is a multifaceted endeavor. The answer

---

[14] Stephen R. Covey, S. R. (2004). *The 7 Habits of Highly Effective People: Restoring the Character Ethic, 15th Anniversary Ed.* (New York: Free Press, 2004).

cannot be found in one place, nor provided by the perspectives of a few employees, no matter how highly placed they may be. The CEO or Vice President of Human Resources may provide *their* appraisal of the organization's DEIB culture and what needs to be done, but it is incumbent upon the DEIB Leader to investigate further and form an objective and honest assessment of whether the organization's words and deeds illustrate a true understanding of and receptiveness to DEIB. Only then can the DEIB Leader design carefully sequenced initiatives that build from the organization's current place on the Journey.

Verbal Commitment

We've seen that the way in which an organization describes its purpose, values, and objectives reveals much about what is important to it. These statements can be found in a variety of writings, including:

- Key governing documents, such as vision and mission statements, listings of core values, and strategic plans.

- Materials created for external stakeholders or required by regulatory agencies, such as annual reports and filings with the Securities and Exchange Commission.

- Information distributed to the workforce: policies, employee handbooks, job descriptions, codes of conduct, and similar resources.

- Website format, messaging, and images.

- Recruiting materials: job postings, job descriptions, applications, position requirements, and promotional literature.

- Sales and marketing materials.

Taken together, these resources form a picture of how the organization sees itself, or at least how it wants to be seen.

With the exception of a strategic plan, this information is readily available to the DEIB Leader. An organization's website frequently includes information about its history, mission, vision, core values, or similar terms under headings like "About Us" or "Who We Are." The words and images it uses, what it includes, what it omits, how many clicks it takes to reach DEIB information—all assist the DEIB Leader in their effort to see the real picture.

As businesses have become more aware of the significance of DEIB, it is not uncommon to find a separate section of a company's website devoted to the organization's beliefs about Diversity, and its self-evaluation of how it is living up to its principles. Terms like "Respect," "Equality," "Diversity," "Inclusion," "Equity," "Opportunity," and other DEIB watchwords may be part of vision and mission statements or included among an organization's core values.

Even organizations that don't employ an explicit DEIB glossary nevertheless include statements that, when viewed through a DEIB lens, can be linked to or aligned with DEIB concepts and practices. And, as seen in our FamilyMeals, Inc. hypothetical, an institution may not be aware that DEIB-related aspirations are part of the path to success that it has charted for itself. A company that touts its "family friendliness" needs to understand "family" as observed from a DEIB perspective before it can increase its reach into the market that includes more than "traditional" families.

An evaluation of a verbal commitment to DEIB is only the first step in determining how far along the DEIB Journey an organization has traveled. Plenty of organizations talk the DEIB talk. After all, little is required to make a verbal commitment to the Principles of Diversity, Equity, Inclusion, and Belonging. However, converting those Principles into practice—*walking the talk*— requires significantly more effort.

Demonstrated Behaviors

These are the actions the organization has taken to advance DEIB beyond words. They are the best indicators of where the organization actually is in embracing and implementing DEIB Principles.

A solid assessment entails a close examination of three areas: Workforce and Marketing Footprint Demographics; Employment Processes and Practices; and External/Community Engagement. Within each category are several subcategories that fill out the DEIB picture.

That said, a review of demonstrated behaviors does not, in and of itself, create a portrait of the organization's DEIB understanding and receptiveness. There are no litmus tests. For instance, simply because Persons of Color comprise a large percentage of an organization's workforce does not in and of itself mean it is inclusive. Nor does the fact that most of the members of its board of directors are female show that its overall environment is welcoming and equitable for women.

A more sophisticated analysis employing a DEIB Lens is needed to tease out salient information. The process entails parsing several interrelated areas. By way of an example, evaluating whether an organization's recruiting practices are consistent with DEIB Principles demands consideration of demographics, sourcing, workforce composition, recruiting materials, and its brand (how it presents itself to the public), among other elements.

WORKFORCE AND MARKETING FOOTPRINT DEMOGRAPHICS

Geographic. What is the makeup of the area in which the organization is located, and/or services? The United States Census Bureau site[15] has a wealth of information. Data includes age, sex, ancestry, race, ethnicity, languages spoken at home, residential mobility, veteran status, income, poverty levels, education, labor force statistics, housing status, disabilities, and families and living arrangements, among others.

In 2020, the Census Bureau also initiated the Household Pulse Survey (HPS). Designed to deploy quickly and efficiently (data is disseminated in near real-time), the survey collects data to measure how emergent issues are impacting U.S. households from a social and economic perspective. It also includes information about some Dimensions of Diversity not reflected in the decennial surveys. For example, in July 2021, the Census Bureau began collecting information on the sexual orientation and gender identity of respondents to the HPS.

Workforce. What is the composition of the organization's workforce? The Human Resource Information System (HRIS) can provide this information. You may need to set up a recurring "Ad Hoc Inclusion Report" tailored to your guidelines once you identify the composition content to ensure timely data as you weave Inclusion reporting into the fabric of the organization.

Management/Decision-Makers. What is the composition of the organization's board of directors, officers, and senior-level managers?

---

[15] The United States Census Bureau. https://www.census.gov/.

Vendors/Suppliers. Who does the organization use to provide the goods and services that it needs to operate internally and externally? This information can be obtained from those at the organization most familiar with its contracting practices. The Census Quickfacts[16] captures a breakdown of all employer firms—men-owned; women-owned; minority-owned; non-minority-owned; veteran-owned; and non-veteran-owned. The National LGBT Chamber of Commerce (NGLCC) is the certifying body of LGBTQ-owned businesses.

Markets/Customers. Where does the organization market and sell its products/services? Who are its customers? Who is purchasing its products/services? Sales and marketing information is the source for the answers to these questions.

EMPLOYMENT PROCESSES AND PRACTICES

Recruitment. Where and how does the organization seek new employees? What are the selected communications vehicles? What is the Attraction and Belonging message? How do job posts align with DEIB Principles?

Retention. What are the demographics of employee turnover? Is the turnover rate significantly higher for certain groups and/or departments?

Benefits. How inclusive are the benefits provided to the workforce? Is the Employee Handbook written with the evolving inclusive or Belonging language?

---

[16] https://www.census.gov/quickfacts/fact/table/US/PST045224.

Pay. How are wage scales (hourly and salaried) set? What is the review process? Who are the decision-makers? How does the organization decide who should receive raises and promotions? If available, pay Equity studies or internal equitable pay analysis can be useful.

Surveys. If employee surveys have been conducted in the past, what, if anything, do the responses reveal about the organization's policies and practices? Were there any culture or inclusivity questions asked? (Forward-looking surveys may be useful in designing and implementing the DEIB Strategic Visioning Framework and are part of the potential measurements of success discussed in Chapter 7.)

Claims. Have any government agencies or employees made claims of discrimination or unfair impact against the organization based upon a Dimension of Diversity (e.g., race, gender, orientation, age, disability)? How recent, frequent, and extensive are the claims? How did the organization respond?

EXTERNAL/COMMUNITY ENGAGEMENT

External engagement. With whom and with which businesses does the organization align and collaborate? Are the organization's external engagements/sponsorships reflecting its current and potential customers?

Community support. What organizations, events, and community activities does the organization support, and to what extent? Does it encourage employees to volunteer on company time?

To recap, how and why an organization has reached its particular place on the DEIB Journey reveals much about its current understanding of and receptiveness to DEIB. An appreciation of the organization's history, as well as where it is currently, enables a DEIB Leader to devise the best solutions for evolving its DEIB practices to reach a sustainable Culture of Belonging.

CHAPTER 7

DEIB STRATEGIC VISIONING FRAMEWORK: DESIGNING FOR GROWTH, SUCCESS, SUSTAINABILITY

Evolution toward a Culture of Belonging can only begin once a carefully crafted DEIB Strategic Visioning Framework has been put in place. Most people we have encountered during our careers have little or no experience with strategic planning. That work is almost exclusively reserved to senior leadership and then driven throughout the organization. Hence, we have included this "how to" chapter to ensure that anyone undertaking DEIB Framework design has a fundamental appreciation for the planning process.

Readers who are well-versed on planning may skim much of this chapter. That said, while some aspects of creating a DEIB Strategic

Visioning Framework do resemble the strategic planning process, they are materially different. We advise that all readers fully absorb these distinctions, as heeding them is crucial to successful DEIB initiatives.

An admonition from Chapter 5 bears repeating: A common mistake that derails DEIB initiatives is the creation of a standalone DEIB strategic plan. *The failure to align DEIB practices with the organization's strategic plan goals is the single greatest reason why DEIB initiatives flounder, never reaching their real potential.* An effective DEIB Strategic Visioning Framework can only be sustainable by aligning DEIB Principles to the organization's existing strategic objectives.

Strategic planning usually begins with a **SWOT analysis,** or examining the organization's Strengths, Weaknesses, Opportunities, and Threats. This and other information are used to inform the creation of the organization's vision, mission, and purpose statements, which are the foundation of the organization.

Strictly speaking, the terms vision, mission, and purpose are different, but they often are used interchangeably, or one is subsumed by the other (usually, purpose is pulled into the mission). A "pure" mission statement succinctly describes how the organization will make its vision a reality. It is intended to be inspirational; LinkedIn's stated mission, for example, is to "Connect the world's professionals to make them more productive and successful." A purpose statement is focused on explaining why the organization exists. Whole Foods tells its employees and the public that "Our purpose is to nourish people and the planet."

Vision, mission, and purpose statements are intended to last for a long time—potentially, the life of the organization. They allow for change without sacrificing the key concepts that led to the reason the organization was created in the first place. As a result, they are brief and deliberately nonspecific.

A DEIB Strategic Visioning Framework does *not* involve the creation of a separate vision, mission, or purpose statement, but exists to help the organization achieve its existing goals, strategies, and tactics that flow from, and are driven by, its stated vision, mission and purpose.

Goals and objectives are what an organization wants to achieve during a given time period. (Goals are sometimes called objectives. We prefer to use "objectives" to avoid confusion with "goals" as used within the context of affirmative action programs.) Strategies are the plans of action to achieve an objective. Tactics are the clearly delineated steps the organization will take to support the strategy; they give life to the strategy. The DEIB Strategic Visioning Framework supports the objectives, strategies, and tactics of the organization's strategic plan.

While an organization has one vision, mission, or purpose, it will almost certainly have multiple objectives, strategies, and tactics as part of the plans it develops across time. An objective may be supported by more than one strategy, each of which may, in turn, drive the creation of several tactics. Put another way, the vision, mission and purpose are constants, while objectives, strategies, and tactics may be modified or replaced across time.

A successful DEIB Framework is one designed with the organization in mind. It will not be based on a template or merely consist of modifications to an existing plan. The Framework design may have its own objectives, strategies, and tactics. There is no standard format.

FRAMEWORK DESIGN PROCESS

While the design of a DEIB Strategic Visioning Framework varies from organization to organization, there are considerations in the design and implementation process that are universally useful. What is most important is that the resulting Framework helps the organization achieve its vision, mission, and identified pillars and/or objectives from the organization's strategic plan in a manner that is aligned with DEIB Principles and practices.

A DEIB Framework is not the same as the strategic planning process conducted by the organization itself or its resulting strategic plan. The DEIB Framework Team gathers information from the organization's existing strategic plan, its SWOT analysis, if one exists, current employee engagement surveys and any other relevant survey results. The team should also review DEIB-related training or discovery learning materials, if any sessions were held, and session evaluation feedback, if any was solicited.

Once the information is digested by the Framework Team, it can prepare an employee survey focused specifically on DEIB. The results of the survey provide a DEIB SWOT analysis for the Framework Team to identify and focus on solution-based initiatives for their Visioning Framework.

The following diagram illustrates the components and flow of the DEIB Framework design process.

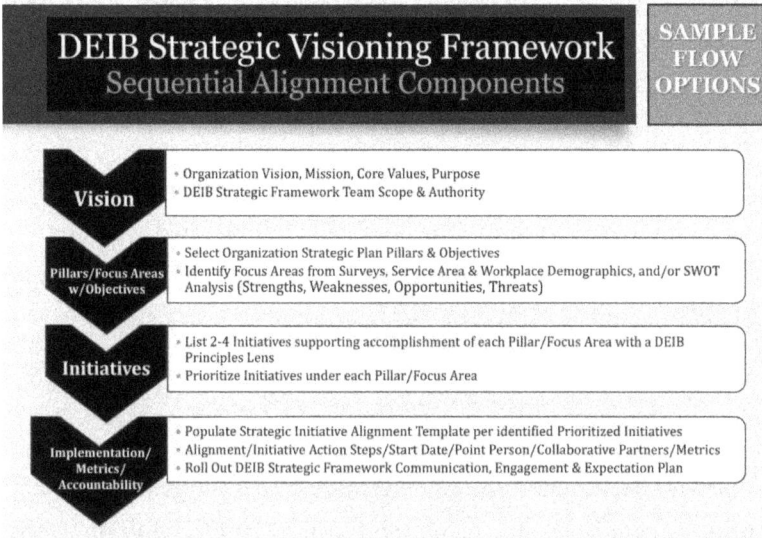

When to Begin the Process

Planning happens *after* acquiring sufficient Organizational Intelligence to design a Framework that meets the organization where it is. Chapter 9 discusses what this entails beyond what we have previously described.

Participants

Any successful Framework requires the input of many resources. Who is selected to be part of the design process has everything to do with both the content and the organization's buy-in when it's time to implement the Framework.

A DEIB Leader must reach across the organization to ensure that all important voices are heard. Those who possess authority or *influence*—the actual decision-makers—should at least be consulted, even if they are not included as part of a formal planning committee. Positioning DEIB allies so that they can help shape the Framework and, even more importantly, foster its implementation, is essential.

Whether an organization already has committees or groups in place that ought to be part of the process should be evaluated. Perspectives of any Inclusion Council and Business Employee Resource Group (BERG) should be captured.

Measuring Success

DEIB metrics enable the organization to assess its progress and build expectations and accountability into its DEIB Framework. In other words, using metrics serves as an acknowledgement that DEIB initiatives will be subject to evaluation in the same manner as any other initiative in the organization. It is another step in making DEIB part of the organization, not an island unto itself. Metrics inform, measure, and drive the implementation of the Framework. Incorporating hard and soft metrics also demonstrates a level of return on investment—"ROI." This reflects the value, seriousness, and confidence that is often missing when plans are created using only high-level aspirational objectives.

Remember that most organizations have little or no experience with DEIB metrics. While they may believe that they should do something about improving their DEIB culture, they are unsure what that means, or what sustainable success looks like.

As the demographics of the organization are easy for it to grasp, it may see DEIB solely as a matter of increasing the diverse representation of the organization's workforce—a "numbers game." This is not only an oversimplification of DEIB, but without educating the organization about the breadth of DEIB and the need to make systemic changes, any improvement in those numbers is likely to be short-lived.

The vast majority of an organization's traditional metrics of success are probably based on internally generated information that has existed for years. Revenue, headcount, subscribers, site visits, and myriad other metrics that organizations utilize to manage and gauge success readily lend themselves to mathematical precision. While some elements of DEIB do as well, others are nuanced. Often, multiple factors must be measured, and the overall metric may be unique to DEIB. New measurement tools will almost certainly be needed to complete planning.

Surveys are another tool for gauging the progress and success of the Framework. They must, of course, be drafted and administered thoughtfully.

Some of the most important questions to ask prior to conducting a survey are:

- What is the appropriate type of survey and name of the contemplated survey? (Engagement, Belonging Culture, Policy, Procedure, Stay, Best Place to Work, Change, New Initiative Input are examples worth considering.)

- What is the right time of year to conduct the survey? What is a realistic length of time to allow for responses?

- "The Questions!" What are the right questions worded in the right way to achieve the end in mind of the survey? Does it capture DEIB questions within the survey (e.g., engagement, culture) in a way to measure the impact of the Framework?

- Are the survey responses being interpreted with an objective and equitable lens?

Ultimately, how the organization will measure progress and success may or may not be included in the wording of specific objectives. This will depend upon how easily metrics can be included without the objective becoming unwieldy or difficult to communicate. It may also be omitted if there is the possibility that it might run afoul of any of the existing or new legal prohibitions against specific targets.

Budget

Potential incremental expenses should be identified whether or not the organization is likely to consider allotting funds earmarked for the DEIB planning process. Will the involvement of non-salaried employees necessitate charges to the cost center where the DEIB planning budget resides? Will any intellectual property or materials from third parties be purchased? Will there be travel or food charges? Approaching the planning process like any other project at the organization demonstrates business acumen. It also fosters greater receptivity by subjecting a DEIB initiative to the same rules as everything else.

Deliverables, Timeline, and Approval

As with any other project at the organization, the DEIB Strategic Visioning Framework requires a deliverable, namely, the Framework

Document, and a timeframe for completion. The Framework Document should include the following:

1. Objectives, with supporting moving-forward initiatives with timeframes;

2. Metrics that help to define objectives and measure progress;

3. Dates by which each objective is to be achieved; and

4. A summary of how the Framework aligns with the organization's vision, mission, core values, and/or a three-to-five-year strategic plan.

To set expectations and drive the planning process across the finish line, a deadline should be established at the outset. Something within a three-to-six-month range is achievable.

Should You Use a Consultant?

Some organizations instinctively turn to an outside consultant to help them with a project initiative where they may lack experience, such as designing a DEIB Strategic Visioning Framework. Before heading in that direction, careful thought should be given to the potential implications of engaging an outside party for this critical task, weighing both the pros and cons.

The use of consultants may enable the organization to draw upon valuable expertise that it lacks. Consultants are also thought to bring a level of objectivity by virtue of the fact that they are not employed by the organization.

On the other hand, a consultant has neither the lived experience of working within the organization's culture nor the personal investment of a DEIB Leader who is also an employee. The organization is but one of the consultant's current clients. The DEIB Leader has more "skin in the game," as they are, and will be, directly affected by the organization's workplace culture and practices. A consultant moves on, looking for more clients.

Additionally, retaining a consultant can be perceived as a lack of confidence and experience on the part of the organization's DEIB Leaders. Why, management may ask, do we need to pay somebody external to the organization to do the job we're already paying specific employees to do? While this is perhaps unfair, especially if the organization routinely hires consultants in other areas, it is a frequent reality of the DEIB Discipline.

Getting a sense of an organization's views on consultants is another aspect of developing Organizational Intelligence. Are they generally frowned upon and viewed as an unnecessary expense? Are they mostly utilized as a defensive maneuver when the organization is looking for an insurance policy in case things don't work out? ("We hired the expert and did what they told us to do . . . it's their fault, not ours.") Or, perhaps, they may be widely accepted as part of how the organization operates.

If an organization decides to proceed with a consultant to help it with designing the DEIB Strategic Visioning Framework, it should establish the appropriate scope of work at the outset. Above all else, it must not give up ownership of the Framework design and implementation. The Framework must be organic, designed specifically for the organization, and understood and supported by its decision-makers. To be sustainable, it cannot be dependent upon an individual or entity outside of the organization.

The Future

The Principles of DEIB are constants. Nevertheless, society is always evolving, as are organizations within that society. We recommend designing your DEIB Strategic Visioning Framework utilizing our 3T Strategic Approach: "Today, Tomorrow, Tweak."

Year 1 is Implementation.

Year 2 is Ensure that Plan processes and metrics are achieving expectations, including being user-friendly to the organization and to the reporting process summaries.

Year 3 is Review Visioning Framework for modifications, replacement, and/or adding new initiatives or tasks.

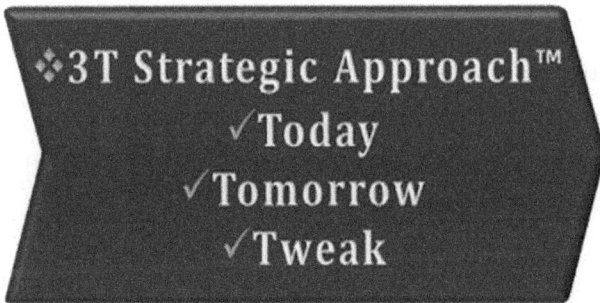

❖3T Strategic Approach™
✓Today
✓Tomorrow
✓Tweak

The Framework should be viewed as a living document. The organization must be on the lookout for changes that necessitate revisions, be they internal or external, to ensure that the Framework remains current and fully aligned. For instance, a new law may allow for the addition of a particular strategy or tactic that helps fulfill an objective. Similarly, legislation could be passed that prohibits or severely limits the organization's ability to employ a specific tactic.

IMPLEMENTATION TIPS

The stakes change dramatically as the organization moves from the Framework design phase to implementation. The risks of drafting strategies and tactics are far less than actuating those design elements. By the same token, this phase is potentially much more exciting. After all, a DEIB Framework without implementation achieves nothing.

Implementation tests the **courage** and commitment of everyone. It is one thing to expect to engage in difficult conversations; it is quite another to have them. Individuals who were vocal supporters of DEIB in general and/or certain strategies or tactics may become reticent when the time arrives to act. Some may claim that they still endorse the approach but feel that the organization "isn't ready" to take that step. Verbal commitment, while a positive, doesn't get the job done. It is only when the words are translated into action that an organization can begin to evolve. Here are some tips for pushing through the resistance that may come.

Anticipate Challenges and Barriers

A DEIB Leader should have a good sense (pulse) of the organization's "hot buttons," including those of individual decision-makers. As they prepare to explain the DEIB Framework to them, the challenges and barriers listed in Chapter 4, "Why Most DEIB Initiatives Have Failed," bear revisiting and referencing as something of a checklist so they can be addressed.

Even better, defuse those concerns before they are articulated. If there are specific challenges that have already been presented, they should be met head-on, rather than waiting to respond to misgivings. It is important to be forward-looking in preparing the landscape for receptiveness prior to introducing the DEIB Strategic Visioning Framework.

Translate the Framework into Concepts that the Organization can Understand

This is key to successful implementation. It is not patronizing; it is critical to help the organization relate to the Framework (continue to "meet them where they are"). Change without understanding is unsustainable. To be willing to move forward with DEIB initiatives, an organization needs to know why they are being recommended and how they will help it accomplish its existing mission, vision, and strategic Framework objectives—in other words, the value and long-term return on its investment (ROI) in the initiatives.

Underscore the Economic Benefits

Instead of positioning DEIB as the right thing to do, an organization is likely to be more enthusiastic about implementation when it is characterized as the Smart Proactive Strategic Approach for Forward-Thinking Growth Minded Organizations! To carry the day with all decision-makers, the DEIB Framework must be linked to tangible benefits for the organization and, indirectly, for them.

Regardless of whether any concerns are raised during implementation, it is wise to look for opportunities to remind the organization that it has adopted the Framework because it is important to its financial objectives and reputation ("Bottom Line and Brand Identity"). These two indicators of success are important to every organization. Both are important to decision-makers on a personal level as well, linked as they are to compensation and promotions.

Advancing the financial advantages of the DEIB Framework is one of the most effective means of getting the organization's attention. These advantages can manifest themselves as increases in revenue or decreases in expenses—the two broad categories that drive the economic performance of any organization. Because both revenue and expenses are expressed in terms of numbers (principally, dollars, but also percentages, when comparing performance across time), there is arguably a measure of objectivity with which most of the organization is comfortable. The metrics help the organization to connect the dots from DEIB to practices that strengthen its financial soundness for today and tomorrow.

Here are a handful of potential illustrations demonstrating value.

- Increase revenue by appealing to a broader market.

- Employee turnover is costly. An inclusive environment where all employees know they belong helps to reduce turnover.

- An inclusive DEIB-savvy work environment is likely to reduce potential claims and fines based upon alleged discrimination or violations of laws that provide protections for all groups.

- A strong DEIB reputation can enhance an organization's brand.

- An Inclusive Environment that fosters a Culture of Belonging enhances team engagement and performance to consistently achieve the best results.

Cultivate Collaborative Partners

Being a DEIB Leader necessitates leading and working with advocates, allies, influencers, sponsors, and mentors, among others. No matter how skilled, a DEIB Leader cannot design and implement a successful DEIB Framework alone. No one can. Not only are there too many components for one person to handle, but the failure to collaborate with others within the organization will doom the Framework to failure.

Power alone is not the sole measure of an individual's potential value. Commitment is a significant part of the equation. While some of the organization's senior executives ought to be part of implementing the Framework, they may not have the most impact on it becoming a reality. Paramount is understanding what the potential impact of a partner can be, and how to leverage their participation in implementation. The DEIB Leader needs to ensure "holistic ownership."

The central purpose of the DEIB Strategic Visioning Framework is to gradually evolve the organization, causing its culture to undergo a metamorphosis that melds DEIB Principles with its existing DNA. Successful implementation weaves DEIB Principles and practices into the fabric of the organization so that they become part of the mosaic that is the entirety of its existence.

How will the organization know that this has happened? When its employees—all of them—begin to demonstrate DEIB-supportive behaviors as much as they do behaviors that support anything else that is important to the organization.

PART 3

TOOLS FOR MOVING FORWARD

CHAPTER 8

THE NEED FOR COURAGE WITH KNOWLEDGE AND AN HONEST SELF-ASSESSMENT

Elizabeth Freeman, Thaddeus Stevens, Harriet Tubman, Elizabeth Peratrovich, Fred Korematsu, Harvey Milk, John Lewis, Richard Loving, Ruby Bridges, Sylvia Rivera, Deborah Parker. These and many more took up the cause for human rights and made a difference. They saw that despite the stated values of the United States of America—"liberty and justice for all," "all men are created equal," and "equal justice under law"—liberty, equality, and justice had in fact been denied to many of its citizens. What's more, these individuals took action, often at risk to their personal safety. They all shared a common trait: **Courage with Knowledge**.

To achieve sustainable change, organizations must empower qualified internal DEIB Leaders to lead them in the systematic implementation of a well-conceived Holistic DEIB Strategic Visioning Framework. Being qualified includes having the courage to engage in uncomfortable dialogue and speak truth to power, when necessary.

Civil rights and social justice advocates, including those listed at the beginning of this chapter, utilized a variety of strategies and tactics. Some acted alone while others worked with like-minded allies, often developing elaborate organizations. Owing to frustration from discrimination and feelings of helplessness, frequently denied access to the institutions they sought to change, many had no choice but to work as outsiders.

The DEIB Leader we describe is someone who is positioned to change an organization from within. They are or will become an employee or board member and live the Principles of DEIB.

Being an effective DEIB Leader is very action-driven. It requires the courage to take risks. It demands being able to affirmatively answer two questions: First, "Do I have the courage with knowledge to lead?" Second, "Do I have the perseverance to do this work, knowing how difficult it is to bring about real and sustainable change?"

THE COURAGE TO LEAD

Why are all the organization's senior officers White men? Are the women receiving pay equal to that of their male counterparts? Are certain ethnic groups disciplined differently than others? What do the workforce demographics look like compared to those of the markets where the organization sells its products or provides services? These and other DEIB topics necessarily involve an examination and discussion of race, ethnicity, gender, age, and other Dimensions of Diversity. Experience teaches that many, if not most, members of U.S. society are very uncomfortable having those discussions.

Indeed, even broaching a topic like race can immediately put people on the defensive. If the White male CEO is asked by the Black Director of Talent Acquisition why his executive team is all White and all male, he is likely to see it as an accusation, not an objective opportunity question. He might feel that the questioner is inferring that he has purposely excluded Persons of Color and Women from his team. Depending upon the circumstances at this organization and length of the CEO's tenure, he may decide that this is a thinly veiled charge of racism and sexism. Tension fills the room. Those witnessing the exchange almost certainly assume that the questioner has managed to draw the CEO's disfavor, perhaps wondering how long the Director will last with the company.

This is but one example of how highly charged even a DEIB-related question can be. We all belong to certain groups. We all have different World Views. Our understanding of and reaction to DEIB topics vary, often dramatically. When beliefs and assumptions are misaligned, a single word can prompt completely different reactions. Within the context of DEIB, for instance, the word **"privilege"** may be seen by the White male CEO differently than the Black Director of Talent Acquisition.

Without doubt, it is easier, or at least more comfortable, to avoid these topics, than to tackle them directly. When the White CEO asks a Black employee if it isn't true that all lives matter, not just Black lives, the employee might very well not respond. It may be because the employee is afraid to appear to be challenging the CEO; the specter of job insecurity—the fear that one may lose a job for going "too far" on

DEIB topics—inhibits what could otherwise be worthwhile exchanges of ideas, understanding, and approaches. Or the employee may simply not know how to articulate what is behind Black Lives Matter as a movement, that all lives won't matter until Black lives do. Instead of shying away from the conversation, though, the DEIB Leader sees this as a teaching opportunity—a leadership opportunity—and does not allow the moment to pass.

The DEIB Leader recognizes that one of their roles is to educate the organization and its decision-makers, so they help to evolve how the organization operates with a DEIB Lens. They may have learned that this CEO believes in creating a diverse and inclusive work environment but doesn't know how to do that. Or they've recognized that the CEO is only paying lip service (verbal commitment only) to DEIB and has been resistant to change. Regardless, the DEIB Leader presses forward and creates an opportunity to inform the CEO about what is behind the creation of Black Lives Matter (informing, educating), knowing that the conversation may be strained.

The tension surrounding DEIB discussions is exacerbated by how difficult it often is to separate the work environment from private life. Telling an employee that their disdain for a member of a particular group cannot be permitted to impact the performance of job duties is quite often seen by that employee as an infringement on their personal beliefs. But refusals to comply and uninformed assertions of legal rights must be addressed, or the organization's ability to create an inclusive workplace is lost then and there (i.e., workplace expectations).

Courage means learning to get comfortable with feeling uncomfortable. It means dealing with situations that become difficult, even stressful. Many of them. It may even lead to concerns about job security.

Become comfortable with being uncomfortable. Being uncomfortable is how we learn, and progress is made. Find clarity in chaos.

The DEIB Leader must be confident that they can adapt to being uncomfortable on a regular basis and not be inhibited from addressing issues and acting. If, despite their genuine commitment to DEIB, their instinct is to back away from difficult situations, and "go along to get along" (for example, because they fear losing their job), they should seriously consider moving over or moving out of the position. Not only are they going to be continuously frustrated, but they are going to do a disservice to both themselves and their organization, and to what all DEIB Leaders are trying to accomplish.

PERSEVERANCE

Even after centuries of fighting for civil and human rights, the advances that have been made have been largely incremental and have come slowly. Evolving an organization toward a Culture of Belonging takes time. Everyone will eventually come on board if they have skin in the game. Why? Because the DEIB Leader has led them there through holistic leadership.

Implementation of the DEIB Strategic Visioning Framework (Chapter 7) may face one challenge after another. The hearts and minds of some employees may not change, but it's a DEIB Leader's responsibility to inform employees of the organization's workplace expectations and demonstrated behaviors aligned to the vision, mission, and core values. Everyone is entitled to their opinions and perspectives, but when you sign on to work within an organization, the expectation is you will live and breathe its mission and values. Change may start slowly, but the pace will pick up as the DEIB Leader—with support from leadership and advocates—informs, educates, and communicates through various vehicles the Holistic Strategic Visioning Framework, in the identified sequential steps.

A DEIB Leader's patience will be tried time and again. But in many circumstances more patience is what is required if there is any hope of changing the organization from within. Planting seeds, explaining DEIB concepts without patronizing the audience, all without becoming frustrated in public, are among the qualities of a DEIB Leader. Remember, a DEIB Leader's end in mind for all the risk-taking and hard work should be to leave a legacy enabling continued systemic change within the organization (DEIB Leader as **Change-Maker**).

SELF-ASSESSMENT

Being a DEIB Leader is difficult and demanding. It's risky. DEIB Leaders are the organization's Chief Challenger(s) to how it conducts itself from a DEIB perspective.

If you believe you are or aspire to be a DEIB Leader, you owe it to yourself and those with whom you work to conduct an honest self-assessment to determine whether you are equipped to work in the DEIB space. You must be realistic and unemotional in your evaluation. Too much is at stake to delude yourself.

If, after some honest soul-searching you conclude that you're ready to move ahead and be a DEIB Leader, it's our fervent hope that this book will positively impact both you and your organization.

"Courage is not the absence of fear but the strength to do what is right in the face of fear."

Courage with Knowledge

Courage, when paired with knowledge, is the ability to act in accordance with one's values and understanding, even when facing fear, difficulty, or potential negative consequences. It's not merely the absence of fear, but the conscious decision to act despite it, informed by the reason and wisdom. This means understanding the potential risks involved and making a deliberate choice to proceed, rather than acting impulsively or recklessly.

Courage is a virtue: It's a strength of character that allows individuals to stand up for what they believe in, pursue their goals, and overcome challenges.

"Role Model The Three Inclusion Enablers: Civility. Respect. Kindness."

(Reference: Glossary)

CHAPTER 9

ORGANIZATIONAL INTELLIGENCE

DEIB touches all aspects of an organization—every division, every department, every employee. Organizational Intelligence, or knowledge of what an organization is all about, is therefore an essential skill of a DEIB Leader. It is a predicate for designing a DEIB Strategic Visioning Framework for the organization so that it *chooses* to integrate DEIB Principles and practices into its operation, not because it is forced to.

Even if an organization supports the idea of becoming more aligned with DEIB Principles, employees may be annoyed, if not outright resistant, if DEIB initiatives are implemented in a way that makes their jobs more difficult. Sound ideas can be unfairly criticized, or ignored altogether, because their presentation failed to take an important aspect of the organization's brand or operation into account. Positioning DEIB as more important than anything else at the organization is bound to engender resentment, creating an otherwise avoidable challenge. A DEIB Strategic Visioning Framework and resulting initiatives are better received when they are presented within a context that reveals an appreciation of the organization's operating realities.

We discuss two components of Organizational Intelligence in previous chapters. In Chapter 5, we provide guidance for uncovering the organization's "Constitution"—the words it uses to define itself internally and to others. Chapter 6, "Meeting An Organization Where It Is," includes methods for discovering the perceptions the organization and its decision-makers have about DEIB. Building upon what we've already shared about Organizational Intelligence, in this chapter we identify and summarize additional facets of this essential tool.

LEARN WHAT THE ORGANIZATION DOES

As important as DEIB is, one must not lose sight of the fact that every organization was established to provide products or services. It was not created to build a model DEIB environment; it isn't in the business of being a paragon of DEIB virtue.

A working knowledge of how the organization functions is necessary to establish credibility and, ultimately, create and implement a DEIB Strategic Visioning Framework that is tailored to the specific needs and demands of the organization. This is not unique to DEIB; anyone in a managerial role that touches multiple aspects of an operation should at least have a fundamental appreciation of what the organization does and how.

Multiple internal and external resources are available to paint a picture of what the organization does. Websites, training videos, sales materials, annual reports, media reports . . . the list is extensive. Soliciting suggestions from department heads and longtime employees also provides a deeper understanding of the organization.

DEIB Leaders should commit to an ongoing effort to better appreciate the environment and industry in which their organization operates. For DEIB Professionals, this is a golden opportunity to meet coworkers and break free of the isolation in which they often find themselves.

The end in mind as DEIB Leaders is to demonstrate a genuine interest in the organization, establishing that DEIB is multidimensional, and its advocates are team players who are trying like everyone else to help the organization succeed. Ideally, with sound Organizational Intelligence a DEIB Leader will be seen not only as a DEIB advocate, but also as someone who applies their expertise to help others achieve their objectives.

LEARN THE ORGANIZATION'S LANGUAGE

CEO, COO, CFO, CLO, CMO, EBITDA (Earnings Before Interest, Taxes, Depreciation, and Amortization), below the line, fiscal year, headcount, RIF (Reduction In Force), market share—to the uninitiated, the language of the world of business is as mysterious and imperceptible as hieroglyphics. Each organization has its own vocabulary and acronyms which it uses internally and within its industry. Many also develop slang, unique terms, or sarcastic references. ("CHAOS" has been used by Safety and Security Departments as a code word for "Corporate Has Arrived On Scene!")

A DEIB Leader needs to be fluent in organization speak. At the most obvious level, a DEIB Leader won't be able to communicate effectively without understanding how the organization talks to itself and to the outside world. Certain words may be loaded with meaning familiar only to insiders. Being able to reach members of the organization in a language with which they are familiar is part of meeting them where they are.

How does one learn the organization's language? Read the organization's internal and external materials, noting words, phrases, acronyms, initialisms, and abbreviations that are unusual or unique. If you're unable to decipher acronyms, initialisms, and abbreviations used inside the organization based upon the context in which they are used, a seasoned employee should be able to shed light on it for you. Some organizations have an acronym glossary, which may be housed on an internal SharePoint.

While not often apparent to the organization, many of its own statements are linked to key DEIB Principles. Therefore, using this language whenever possible helps the organization learn how to hold itself accountable to its own values and objectives. For example, consider "We should sponsor this community event as it aligns with our giving approach of hunger and kids." Connecting an organization's words to its behavior enables it to **"walk the talk."**

LEARN WHO REALLY MAKES DECISIONS

Most organizations are structured as a hierarchy. However, the use of titles often obscures how decisions are made. To discern who holds real power, one must look beyond the organizational chart and use keen observational skills, active listening, and political savvy. There is no handbook or memo listing the most influential board member, or who in Operations is often consulted by the CEO.

To be sure, one must be cognizant of the reporting and departmental structure in place to ascertain how important that structure is to how decisions are made. Some organizations observe a strict etiquette driven by an "official chain of command" structure, while others are less formal.

It is not uncommon to find that several of the most influential, and therefore powerful, people in an organization are not part of the upper echelon of the organization's hierarchy. Who are the people who really make things happen at the organization? Who are the influencers who always seem to have a role in significant decisions? Who do those who have the most power listen to?

Additionally, where does power reside within the organization's groupings? For instance, while all Vice Presidents are equals by virtue of a shared title, it is almost certain that some hold greater power than others. This may be because the area they oversee is more highly valued than another. Finance may be treated as being more important than Marketing, for example. Or they may hold greater sway over the organization because they are simply more competent at organizational politics than their counterparts.

The components of Organizational Intelligence that we've described thus far are arguably salient for any employee who wants to succeed. However, there are two more that are required for those intent upon becoming a DEIB Leader: a degree of business acumen, and the ability to assess the organization's perceptions of and current alignment with DEIB Principles and practices. Both of these are necessary to enable a DEIB Leader to effectively educate and influence an organization.

BUSINESS ACUMEN

In its earliest days, DEIB was largely seen as an add-on to Human Resources' responsibilities. It is, unfortunately, frequently seen as a "soft skill" or administrative aspect of running an organization that adds little or nothing to its bottom-line profitability or other measures of success. While many CEOs tout people as being the organization's most important asset, the departments and employees tasked with managing "people issues" rarely, if ever, carry the most weight when it comes to moving the organization in a particular direction. Human Resources frequently can be incorrectly viewed as an "expense" rather than a "profit" department.

Why? Because so many measures of success are expressed in numbers, which are thought to be objective. Sales, revenue, profit margins, and market penetration all readily translate into dollars and percentages. Never mind that numbers can be manipulated ("figures lie and liars figure"), the coin of the realm for most organizations is achievement as measured by numbers.

This is where the organization is, so a DEIB Leader must develop a basic understanding of the business of the organization, whether it is a for-profit or non-profit entity. This is not to say that one must learn the nuances of Generally Accepted Accounting Principles (GAAP) or how to compute EBITDA. But a working knowledge of key business concepts at a high level is essential. Beyond that, an awareness of the concepts that are most important to the organization (e.g., revenue and expenses; balance sheet basics; significant regulatory, legal, and political issues), and why they are important is valuable Organizational Intelligence.

Several of our tips mentioned in Chapter 7 for successfully designing and implementing a DEIB Strategic Visioning Framework are dependent upon an ability to articulate and measure the impact of the Framework and its related initiatives. The business-related purpose and value-add of those initiatives should be articulated.

PERCEPTIONS AND ALIGNMENT

Chapter 6, "Meeting An Organization Where It Is," explains this component.

Once a DEIB Leader has attained Organizational Intelligence, they will be positioned to help the organization evolve by voluntarily weaving DEIB best practices into its operations. In this way, the organization can come to understand that it is not being asked to change *per se*. Rather, it is learning to hold itself accountable to its own objectives and values with a forward-thinking DEIB Lens.

CHAPTER 10

EVOLVING U.S. POPULATION DEMOGRAPHICS

The most effective DEIB approach is to focus on systematically implementing sustainable, solution-oriented processes that are integral to humanity and achieving the best performance. These processes, built upon DEIB Principles and tools, will strengthen forward-thinking organizations for both the short- and long-term.

It is crucial for DEIB Leaders to be the "informed clarity leaders" and facilitate clear communication within their entities. They need to connect the dots to the evolving population demographics within the United States, specifically, the organization's service area footprint and internal workforce, to reflect those whom the organization serves.

DEMOGRAPHICS[17]

During the twenty-first century the U.S. has seen several demographic turning points.

- The United States Census Population Growth from 2000 to 2010 was 9.7 percent.

- The United States Census Population Growth from 2010 to 2020 was 7.4 percent.

- The 2020 Census Data reveals Children of Color represent a 53 percent majority share of the U.S. child population, and non-Hispanic White Children make up 47.3 percent.

- The Diversity among children[18] is a result of two trends: an increase in the Children of Color population and a decrease in the non-Hispanic White child population.

- The 2021 combined **buying power** of African Americans, Asian Americans, and Native Americans was $3.2 trillion, while the nation's Hispanics commanded $2.1 trillion in

---

[17] Data for Chapter 9 from: United States Census Bureau, "Demographic Turning Points for the United States: Population Projections for 2020 to 2060," https://www.census.gov/content/dam/Census/library/publications/2020/demo/p25-1144.pdf; United States Census Bureau QuickFacts https://www.census.gov/quickfacts/fact/table/US/PST045224.

[18] For U.S. Children, Minorities Will Be The Majority By 2020, Census Says, https://www.npr.org/sections/thetwo-way/2015/03/04/390672196/for-u-s-children-minorities-will-be-the-majority-by-2020-census-says; United States Census Bureau https://data.census.gov/table/ACSDP5Y2010.DP05?q=2010+frederick+county+maryland++population+demographics.

spending power—larger than the Gross Domestic Product (GDP) of Australia.

- Nearly 17.5 percent of buying power in the U.S. belongs to African American, Asian American, and Native American households. That equates to nearly $1 out of every $5.75 of buying power in the U.S.

United States population demographics and expectations are rapidly evolving and the ineffectiveness of a "one-size-fits-all" approach or strategy has become even more apparent. The year 2030 marks a demographic turning point for the country. Beginning that year, all baby boomers will be older than sixty-five and, within the decade, older adults (sixty-five years and older) are projected to outnumber children (under eighteen years) for the first time in U.S. history.

The U.S. population is also projected to experience several additional demographic milestones by *2060*. As the population grows slowly and ages considerably, it will become significantly more racially and ethnically pluralistic.

ADJUSTING THE ORGANIZATION'S DEMOGRAPHIC LENS

To more fully understand why the U.S. economic picture is changing, organizations should be made aware of significant demographic trends. For instance, the "two or more races" population is projected to be the fastest growing over the next forty-six years. Outdated one-size-fits-all financial analytics based upon the spending habits of homogeneous demographic groups have become unreliable as new intergenerational and multicultural segments of the population emerge.

An appreciation for generational differences is especially important for an organization. It helps it to better understand and manage its workforce, for one. Marketing and product/service development need to be equipped to address the different preferences of multiple generations.

For example, millennials (born between 1981 and 1996) are the largest adult generation in the United States (though they are starting to share the spotlight with Generation Z (born between 1997 and 2012). Millennials are more educated, more racially and ethnically diverse, and slower to marry than previous generations were at the same age. Each generation has a set of core values and expectations in our ever-evolving world.

Generations Defined By Name
(Generalization Cohorts = Labeling)

Generation	Year Born	Engagement Belonging Value	
▷ Generation Beta	2025 - 2039	TBD	If you do some research, you'll find that dates overlap, and names vary. While we hear generational terms all the time, the definitions are not official. However, based on widespread consensus as well as new Gen Z analysis by the Pew Research Center, and the one generation defined by the U.S. Census Bureau (Baby Boomers), these are the birth years of the generations you'll currently want to use.
▷ Gen Alpha	2013 - 2024	Equity & Parity Fairness	
Gen Z	1997 - 2012		
▷ Millennials (Gen Y)	1981 - 1996	Lives Inclusion	
▷ Gen X ↘	1965 - 1980	Practices Diversity	
▷ Boomers (Sandwich)	1946 - 1964	Civil Rights	
Post War (Silent/Traditionalist)	1928 - 1945	The Veterans Loyalty Country/Company/Family	
▷ WW II (Greatest Generation)	1901 - 1927		

Age Range by Generation | Beresford Research
Where Millennials end and Generation Z begins | Pew Research Center

A DEIB Leader should educate their organization about evolving demographics and help it adapt. Their knowledge can assist managers and Human Resources executives in developing multigenerational strategies in recruitment, new hire orientation, talent management, retention, leadership engagement, navigation skills, and succession planning.

LOOKING AHEAD

The United States population is expected to rise to approximately *380 million* by *2050*. This projection assumes that currently observed population trends will continue. Between 2005 and 2050, 82 percent of this population growth is predicted to be from immigrants and their descendants. This means that sixty-seven million people will be added to the population from immigrants, forty-seven million people will be added from second-generation immigrants, and three million from third-generation immigrants. In total, 19 percent of the country's residents in 2050 are expected to be foreign-born.

The racial makeup of the United States in 2050 is projected to greatly contrast that of the early 2000s. Nearly half (47 percent) of the population will be non-Hispanic Whites; 29 percent will be Hispanics; and 5 percent of the population will be of Asian descent. From 2005 to 2050 the Black population will remain approximately the same at 13 percent.

Age is another key factor to look at in population projections for 2050. The current trend of population aging will have an increasingly significant impact in the coming years. By 2050, 22 percent of the population will be 65 and older; in 2014, this age group made up 15 percent of the population. The eighteen to sixty-four age group will comprise 58 percent of the population, and the under eighteen group will make up 20 percent.

Paying attention to population demographics is an important tool for any DEIB Leader on many levels. Among other things, this information helps to inform the design of the DEIB Strategic Visioning Framework. It is important that an organization's employees be comfortable working with colleagues, customers, patients, and/or clients from diverse cultural backgrounds. These statistics make it imperative that the organization is equipped to not only welcome Diversity within the organization but also show employees how to navigate an increasingly racially, ethnically, and socioeconomically diverse society and global economy.

Demographic Turning Points

- The year **2030** marks a demographic turning point for the United States. Beginning that year all baby boomers will be older than 65 and, within the decade, older adults (65 years and older) are projected to outnumber children (under 18 years) for the **first time** in U.S. history.

- U.S. population is projected to experience several demographic milestones by **2060**, as the population grows slowly, ages considerably, and becomes more racially and ethnically pluralistic.

Demographic Turning Points for the United Sates: Population Projections for 2020 to 2060 (census.gov)

CHAPTER 11

CALL TO ACTION

Now it's time to apply lessons learned to your role as a DEIB Leader, whether or not DEIB is part of your job description. By being a Proactive Forward-Thinking DEIB Leader, you can leverage your position at your organization, whatever it may be, to advance DEIB Principles and help the organization evolve toward a Culture of Belonging for everyone.

As you consider how best to convert what you've learned from this book into action, we suggest that you keep these observations and suggestions in mind:

Consistently Recognize the Total Sum of the Person. Always remember that all human beings possess multiple Dimensions of Diversity and should be seen and valued for the totality of who they are, not as a single specific dimension.

Focus on Impactful Systemic Changes. Devote your time and energy to DEIB initiatives that are sustainable and have a long-term effect on how the organization functions. Try to avoid one-offs that provide momentary recognition for the organization, but not a lasting impact.

Be Intentional and Embrace the Holistic Change-Maker Role of a DEIB Leader. Seek out opportunities to help your organization move forward on its DEIB Journey in the wide array of areas that impact its culture, such as policies, processes, and procedures; recruitment and retention; onboarding and trainings; pay Equity; succession planning; vendor and supplier sourcing; communication and marketing approach, including website and other media imaging choices; authentic community engagement; bi/multi-language use; and salient professional development, such as learning how to be a **Holistic Leader**.

Commit to Preparation. Do the work that is required to develop Organizational Intelligence and create a sustainable DEIB Strategic Visioning Framework. There are no shortcuts to achieving long-term sustainability.

Have Courage with Knowledge. Confront challenging situations. Take risks when necessary. Give yourself permission to become comfortable with being uncomfortable; remember that is how human beings learn, grow, and progress.

Practice Determination and Perseverance with Reasonable Patience. Reasonable patience is more likely to engender receptiveness than exasperation. It need not be inexhaustible, though. If you must be insistent, use Organizational Intelligence to do so in a way that minimizes adverse impacts on the implementation of the DEIB Strategic Visioning Framework or specific initiatives at the center of the organization's resistance.

Understand Your Lens and Try to Understand the Lens of Others. Be self-aware about your own lived experiences and how you see the world. When working with others as a DEIB Leader, seek first to understand them and their perspective (meet them where they are), then to be understood.

Commit to Ongoing Learning. While DEIB Principles are constants, the environment in which your organization and you operate is always evolving. Stay abreast of new and repealed laws, events, demographics, research, and other information that impacts DEIB initiatives, and your organization's DEIB Strategic Visioning Framework in particular.

Sharpen Your Communication Skills. Continuously improve your writing, active listening, and verbal capabilities to effectively connect the DEIB dots to what is important to your organization and translate those concepts into user-friendly words that it can understand, and utilize your varied communication tools.

Every Contribution is Helpful. You don't have to be a DEIB expert, lawyer, or part of the Human Resources Department to be a positive DEIB influence on your organization. Every time you advocate for DEIB Principles, or support them through your demonstrated behaviors, you are having a beneficial influence on your organization. You may not even realize when you are planting a seed of understanding with a coworker who may one day become a DEIB Leader themselves.

It's Not Complicated. The heart of DEIB is simple: all of humanity wants to be valued and be treated like they belong in the society in which they live. This wisdom acts as an anchor when one becomes overwhelmed by the challenges of trying to establish the Society norms of Mutual Respect, Civility, and Fairness.

ACT! Walk the Talk. Do at least one positive DEIB-related action at your organization every day.

It is our passionate aspiration that you will embrace the twenty-five-year tested new way of thinking about DEIB laid out in this book to help your organization advance toward a sustainable Culture of Belonging. Thank you in advance for your contributions to weaving DEIB Principles into the norms of your organization and our society. Thank you for being receptive to Unlearn and Relearn A New Approach to move our country forward.

Leave a Systemic Change Legacy!

Wishing You Much Success,

Deborah and Frank

GLOSSARY

It is crucial for DEIB Leaders to be the "informed clarity leaders" and facilitate clear communication within their organizations, especially regarding undefined letters and acronyms. It's time to bring clarity to the words you select for today and tomorrow. Focus on systematically implementing sustainable, solution-oriented processes that are integral to Humanity and achieving Best Performance. These processes, built upon DEIB Principles and tools, will strengthen forward-thinking organizations for short- and long-term success.

TERM	DEFINED
AFFIRMATIVE ACTION	• Policies, legislation, programs, and procedures to improve the educational or employment opportunities of members of a certain demographic as a remedy to the effects of long-standing discrimination against such groups.
BARRIER	• An obstruction, obstacle, or other restriction that one may not be able to overcome because the necessary response is outside their decision-making authority or control (as distinguished from a challenge). • That which you may not have direct control of or authority to remove but must be aware of and plan for when developing strategies and implementation.
BELONGING	• Feeling of being accepted, respected, and valued as part of a community. It's about fostering a culture where individuals *know* they can bring their whole selves to work and contribute meaningfully.

TERM	DEFINED
CULTURE OF BELONGING	• The sense of belonging occurs when the person knows that they are part of something bigger than themselves and, therefore, recognizes the rest of the members of their reference group as equals. This can have a very positive effect on their self-esteem, and it is especially important for younger generations. • Feeling of being taken in and accepted as part of a group, thus fostering a sense of belonging. • It also relates to being approved of and accepted by society in general. • Also called belongingness.
BUYING POWER	Consumer Buying Power is an individual's total income after paying taxes.
CHALLENGE	• A difficulty, hindrance, hurdle, or stumbling block that may be overcome with a response that is within your decision-making authority or control (as distinguished from a barrier). • Anything that calls for special effort. • A test of one's abilities or resources in a demanding but stimulating undertaking.
CHANGE-MAKER	Someone who: • Is comfortable out of their comfort zone and understands the value and the need to proactively go to those places. • Desires change in the world and, by gathering knowledge and resources, makes that change happen. • Is driven by partnering with others, being creative, and developing solutions. • Is value driven, mission driven, and thrives on meaningful action for purpose, on purpose. • Is deeply passionate about solving a particular issue or a problem for the purpose of the greater good. A Change-Maker often is highly empathetic and idealistic. • Passionately working on a hopeful mission, no matter how difficult the obstacles or circumstances.

TERM	DEFINED
CIVILITY	• Claiming and caring for one's identity, needs, and beliefs without degrading someone else's in the process. • Disagreeing without disrespect, seeking common ground as a starting point for dialogue about differences, listening past one's preconceptions, and teaching others to do the same. • Being courteous; politeness; a polite action or expression.
CIVIL RIGHTS LAWS	• Civil rights are the rights of citizens to political and social freedom and equality. These include laws guaranteeing equal opportunities and protection under the law, regardless of race, religion, and other Dimensions of Diversity. Many Civil Rights Laws have been enacted since the United States was formed, including as amendments to the U.S. Constitution. • Contemporary reference to Civil Rights Laws in the U.S. refers to those laws impacting civil rights (including voting, housing, and employment) that were enacted during the period from the late 1950s (Civil Rights Act of 1957) to the present. For additional information: https://history.house.gov/Exhibitions-and Publications/BAIC/Historical-Data/Constitutional-Amendments-and-Legislation/
COURAGE	• "Courage is not the absence of fear but the strength to do what is right in the face of fear." ~ Anonymous See Chapter 8 for additional information about courage within the context of DEIB.
COURAGE WITH KNOWLEDGE	• Courage, when paired with knowledge, is the ability to act in accordance with one's values and understanding, even when facing fear, difficulty, or potential negative consequences. It's not merely the absence of fear, but the conscious decision to act despite it, informed by reason and wisdom. This means understanding the potential risks involved and making a deliberate choice to proceed, rather than acting impulsively or recklessly. • Courage is a virtue: It's a strength of character that allows individuals to stand up for what they believe in, pursue their goals, and overcome challenges.

TERM	DEFINED

DEIB
 	
(DIVERSITY, EQUITY, INCLUSION, BELONGING)
	• ACRONYM for Diversity, Equity, Inclusion, & Belonging.
	
	• DEIB IS ABOUT HUMANITY: You and Me, All of Us *(e pluribus unum – out of many, one)*
	  ➤ All human beings possess multiple Dimensions of Diversity.
	  ➤ How we treat and value each other. Mutual respect, fairness.
	  ➤ The principle of valuing each individual's knowledge, abilities, lived experience, and creativity (what one brings to the table).
	
	• DEIB INCLUDES the deliberate, organized, and sustained actions necessary to educate organizations . . . about the many dimensions of Diversity, . . . and help them identify and adopt behaviors and practices that: bring traditionally excluded individuals and groups into processes, activities, and decision/policymaking in a way that shares value and power and ensures equal access to opportunities and resources (Inclusion)."
	
	• DEIB IS NOT
	  ➤ Solely about race, gender, hue of skin, or socioeconomics
	  ➤ About placing blame for the past mistreatment of various groups or trying to rewrite U.S. history
	  ➤ About "bashing" White males
	  ➤ Compliance
	  ➤ Affirmative action
	  ➤ "Reverse discrimination"
	  ➤ Unconstitutional
	  ➤ Illegal
	  ➤ A zero-sum proposition
	  ➤ A siloing, separating, or stand-alone concept
	  ➤ Having to look like me, sound like me, think like me, have gone to the same school as me in order to be a "good fit"

TERM	DEFINED
DEIB APPROACH	• A holistic approach to systematically weaving the Principles of DEIB into an organization's culture by aligning DEIB Principles with its mission, vision, core values, and strategic objectives. A holistic approach teaches that DEIB Principles must be implemented strategically and sequentially for sustainable culture change. • The forward-thinking, smart, and proactive systemic change principle of connecting the dots to what is important to an organization and aligning their brand identity marketing words to show the value of Inclusion.
DEIB LEADER	An individual who supports and lives the Principles of Diversity, Equity, Inclusion, and Belonging (DEIB) from a holistic perspective. They view every aspect of their work broadly and strategically, considering the current and future impact on the entire organization, offering sustainable solutions built upon DEIB Principles and concepts that strengthen the organization for both the short-term and the long-term. They possess the qualities, substantive expertise, and interpersonal skills essential for becoming an effective DEIB Leader: courage with knowledge, perseverance, organizational intelligence, a DEIB Lens, and command of evolving DEIB terminology and demographics.
DEIB LENS	• Seeing things in a way that takes the Principles of DEIB into consideration. See Chapter 5 and the FamilyMeals, Inc. hypothetical as an example.
DEIB PRINCIPLES	DEIB is about Humanity: You and Me, All of Us. Its three Principles are straightforward and beneficial to every member of society. 1. All human beings possess multiple Dimensions of Diversity and should be *seen* and *valued* for the totality of who they are, not as one or a few specific dimensions. ➢ Being *seen* is about the "imbedded Dimensions of Diversity" that are easily perceived by others: race, ethnicity, hue of skin, accent, gender, disability, religion, height, weight, for example.

TERM	DEFINED
	➢ Being *valued* is about the *"authentic* diversity dimensions" that others do not easily perceive without being receptive to engage: knowledge, abilities, lived experience, creativity, and several more.
	2. All members of society should treat one another with mutual respect and fairness.
	➢ "Society" includes individuals, as well as government institutions and other organizations comprised of a collection of individuals.
	3. Put into practice the three Inclusion Enablers of civility, respect, and kindness.
	➢ These Enablers should be engrained into the norms of U.S. society
	Reference their individual definitions within this Glossary.
DIMENSIONS OF DIVERSITY	• Age • Communication styles • Disability/Capability/Accessibility • Gender, Sexual Orientation, Gender Identity, Gender Expression • Generations • Geography • Healthcare Status, Sense of Wellness • Lived Experience • Multiculturalism • Race, Ethnicity, Hue of Skin • Religion • Skills, Knowledge

TERM	DEFINED
	• Socioeconomics (wealth, upper income, middle class, lower income, working poor, poverty, below poverty) • Values, Perspectives, Ideas • Veterans
DIVERSITY	• All the ways in which we are unique; the *total sum* of the person. • As human beings with different lived experiences we naturally have more than just one dimension/identifier. • Difference is natural—*no one has your fingerprints!* • Managing diversity is a working together process for fostering a comfortable environment that works for everyone.
DNA *(As it Pertains to an Organization or Societal Norms)*	• Organizational DNA refers to the underlying characteristics that define an organization's culture, personality, and behavior, much like biological DNA dictates the traits of a living organism. It encompasses the core values, beliefs, and unwritten rules that shape how the organization operates and interacts with its environment. Understanding an organization's DNA is crucial for aligning strategy, improving performance, and fostering a healthy organizational culture.
EEOC	• The Equal Employment Opportunity Commission of the United States. https://www.eeoc.gov/overview
EEO CLASSIFICATIONS Equal Employment Opportunity Classifications *(EEO/USA)* *Also Used in Census Data*	IN PLACE AS OF MARCH 27, 2024 • **EEO definitions of Race/Color/National Origin (also used in U.S Census Data):** ➤ **American Indian/Native Indian/Alaska Native (Indigenous)** ▪ All persons having origins in any of the original peoples of North, Central, or South America, and maintain tribal/community affiliations

TERM	DEFINED
	➤ **Asian/Asian Indian/Indian American** ▪ All persons having origins in any of the original peoples of the Far East, Southeast Asia ▪ This area includes, for example: China, Japan, Korea, Vietnam, India ➤ **Black/African American** ▪ All persons having origins in any of the original peoples of the Black racial groups ▪ This area includes, for example: African American, African, South Africa, Jamaica, Caribbean, Haiti, West Indies ➤ **Hispanic/Latino** ▪ All persons of Mexican, Puerto Rican, Cuban, Central or South American, or other Spanish Culture or origin, regardless of race ➤ **Native Hawaiian/Other Pacific Islander** ▪ All persons having origins in any of the original peoples of the Pacific Islands ▪ This area includes, for example: Hawaii, Philippine Islands, Samoa ➤ **White/Caucasian/Anglo** ▪ All persons having origins in any of the original peoples of Europe, North Africa, or in the Middle East ➤ **Two or More Races** ▪ All persons having a combination of origins in any of the above https://www.eeoc.gov/statutes/title-vii-civil-rights-act-1964

TERM	DEFINED
EEO CLASSIFICATIONS **Revised Statistical Policy Directive No. 15** **Equal Employment Opportunity Classifications** *(EEO/USA)* *Also Used in Census Data*	**EFFECTIVE MARCH 28, 2024** **IMPLEMENTED NOT LATER THAN** *MARCH 28, 2029* • The Office of Management and Budget (OMB) is announcing revisions to Statistical Policy Directive No. 15: Standards for Maintaining, Collecting, and Presenting Federal Data on Race and Ethnicity (SPD 15). • The provisions of these standards are *effective March 28, 2024* for all new record keeping or reporting requirements that include racial or ethnic information. All existing record keeping or reporting requirements should be made consistent with these standards through a non-substantive change request to the Office of Information and Regulatory Affairs (OIRA), or at any time a collection of information is submitted to OIRA for approval of either a revision or extension under the Paperwork Reduction Act of 1995 (PRA), as soon as possible, *but not later than March 28, 2029.* *Example.* The following figure provides an illustrative example of a question format that complies with SPD 15. The standards do not specify the order that responses must be presented, but agencies typically order the responses alphabetically, as shown, or by population size. SPD 15 envisions that whenever possible agencies will collect race and ethnicity data with a question format that includes the required minimum categories disaggregated by the required detailed categories as illustrated in Figure 1.[19]

---

[19] https://www.federalregister.gov/documents/2024/03/29/2024-06469/revisions-to-ombs-statistical-policy-directive-no-15-standards-for-maintaining-collecting-and; https://www.federalregister.gov/d/2024-06469/page-22193.

TERM	DEFINED
	What is your race and/or ethnicity? _Select all that apply_ and enter additional details in the spaces below. ☐ **American Indian or Alaska Native** – _Enter, for example, Navajo Nation, Blackfeet Tribe of the Blackfeet Indian Reservation of Montana, Native Village of Barrow Inupiat Traditional Government, Nome Eskimo Community, Aztec, Maya, etc._ ☐ **Asian** – _Provide details below._ ☐ Chinese ☐ Asian Indian ☐ Filipino ☐ Vietnamese ☐ Korean ☐ Japanese _Enter, for example, Pakistani, Hmong, Afghan, etc._ ☐ **Black or African American** – _Provide details below._ ☐ African American ☐ Jamaican ☐ Haitian ☐ Nigerian ☐ Ethiopian ☐ Somali _Enter, for example, Trinidadian and Tobagonian, Ghanaian, Congolese, etc._ ☐ **Hispanic or Latino** – _Provide details below._ ☐ Mexican ☐ Puerto Rican ☐ Salvadoran ☐ Cuban ☐ Dominican ☐ Guatemalan _Enter, for example, Colombian, Honduran, Spaniard, etc._ ☐ **Middle Eastern or North African** – _Provide details below._ ☐ Lebanese ☐ Iranian ☐ Egyptian ☐ Syrian ☐ Iraqi ☐ Israeli _Enter, for example, Moroccan, Yemeni, Kurdish, etc._ ☐ **Native Hawaiian or Pacific Islander** – _Provide details below._ ☐ Native Hawaiian ☐ Samoan ☐ Chamorro ☐ Tongan ☐ Fijian ☐ Marshallese _Enter, for example, Chuukese, Palauan, Tahitian, etc._ ☐ **White** – _Provide details below._ ☐ English ☐ German ☐ Irish ☐ Italian ☐ Polish ☐ Scottish _Enter, for example, French, Swedish, Norwegian, etc._ _Figure 1._ https://www.federalregister.gov/documents/2024/ 03/29/2024-06469/revisions-to-ombs-statistical- policy-directive-no-15-standards-for-maintaining- collecting-and; https://www.federalregister. gov/d/2024-06469/page-22193
EQUAL EMPLOYMENT OPPORTUNITY LAWS	• Federal laws that make it illegal to discriminate against a job applicant or an employee because of a characteristic of the person that is protected by law.

TERM	DEFINED
(Federal EEOC)	• Equal Employment Opportunity: The law prohibits discrimination in all aspects of employment, including recruitment, selection, evaluation, promotion, training, compensation, discipline, retention, scheduling, and working conditions. • Federal EEO laws do not require an employer to extend preferential treatment to any person or group because of race, color, religion, sex, national origin, age, or handicapping condition [disability]. • EEO merely demands that all persons receive the same opportunities for learning, hiring, training, promotion, etc. • These laws protect individuals by prohibiting discrimination on the basis of: ➢ Race, color (hue of skin and tone) ➢ Religion, (sincerely held beliefs and practices) ➢ Sex (including transgender status, sexual orientation, and pregnancy), (Equal Pay Act) ➢ National origin, ethnicity (ancestors) ➢ Disability, (visible or invisible physical/mental/emotional) ➢ Age (forty or older) ➢ Genetic information, (see individual definition within Glossary) ➢ Retaliation ■ It is also illegal to retaliate against a person because he or she complained about discrimination, filed a charge of discrimination, or participated in an employment discrimination investigation or lawsuit. See, for example, Title VII of the Civil Rights Act of 1964, eeoc.gov/statutes/title-vii-civil-rights-act-1964, and Prohibited Employment Poicies/Practices, eeoc.gov/prohibited-employment-policiespractices

TERM	DEFINED
END IN MIND	• Begin With the End in Mind is based on imagination—the ability to envision in your mind what you cannot at present see with your eyes. It is based on the principle that all things are created twice. There is a mental (first) creation, and a physical (second) creation. Physical creation follows the mental, just as a building follows a blueprint. For additional information see the discussion of Habit 2 "Begin With The End In Mind" in the *7 Habits of Highly Effective People* Covey, S. R. (2004). New York: Free Press.
EQUAL/EQUALITY	• The state of being equal, especially in status, rights, and opportunities. • *Best definition* for Equality: ➢ Equality is about ensuring that every individual has an equal opportunity to make the most of their lives and talents ➢ It is also the belief that no one should have poorer life changes because of how they were assigned at birth, where they come from, what they believe, or whether they have a disability ➢ The Three categories of Equal/Equality: ▪ Social ▪ Economic ▪ Political
EQUITY	A behavioral tool for quickly and easily establishing a society where all groups are genuinely equal. "Equity" speaks to the condition of a society as a whole, not just individuals as compared to other individuals. It consists of fairness, impartiality, and genuine access to the same opportunities. The "perceived" square becomes part of the belonging circle.

TERM	DEFINED
EXPANDING THE TABLE	• Ultimately, Expanding The Table from an Inclusionary Lens (no one is replaced, no one loses their seat at the table) is about building a truly equitable and inclusive environment where *everyone* has a seat, a voice, and a sense of belonging. This not only benefits the individuals involved but also strengthens the organization or community as a whole through enhanced creativity, better decision-making, and a more vibrant and engaged environment. This approach enables higher team performance to achieve the Best Results or Outcomes.
	• Expanding The Table means more than simply having a diverse representation of people present. Instead, it entails actively creating an inclusive environment where everyone's unique perspectives that come from diverse backgrounds, including different cultures, communication styles, lived experiences, and neurodiverse thinking experiences, are genuinely valued, heard, and empowered to contribute meaningfully to the conversation and decision-making processes.
GENETIC INFORMATION (GINA)	• Title II of the Genetic Information Nondiscrimination Act of 2008 (GINA) protects applicants and employees from discrimination based on genetic information in hiring, promotion, discharge, pay, fringe benefits, job training, classification, referral, and other aspects of employment. GINA also restricts employers' acquisition of genetic information and strictly limits disclosure of genetic information. Genetic information includes information about genetic tests of applicants, employees, or their family members; the manifestation of diseases or disorders in family members (family medical history); and requests for or receipt of genetic services by applicants, employees, or their family members.
HOLISTIC APPROACH	• A methodology based on the perspective that the parts of something are interconnected and can be explained only by reference to the whole; the solution demands a holistic approach and a strategic vision of what can be achieved.

TERM	DEFINED
	• Considering all interconnected aspects of a system or situation as a whole, rather than focusing on isolated parts, emphasizing the interconnectedness and interdependence of elements. A DEIB Strategic Visioning Framework must encompass the entire organization, entity, campus, etc.; not just one department, division, or region.
HOLISTIC LEADER	• Someone who recognizes and addresses the interconnectedness of the individuals, teams, and the broader environment to foster sustainable success. They prioritize the well-being and development of their team members, considering not only their professional tasks but also their emotional, physical, and spiritual needs. • This approach emphasizes collaboration, empathy, and a balanced perspective, leading to a more engaged, productive, and thriving work environment.
INCLUSION	• "Seeing The 'Me' In 'We' " • Cultivating an inclusive culture that embraces our differences in experiences, backgrounds, and perspectives. • The act of encouraging belonging. • Ensuring the part is embraced in the whole. • Taking everything and everyone into account. • Ensuring all associates (employees, students, patients, team members, stakeholders, etc.) feel valued. • It does not matter if you are different; each person has the same opportunities. • Creating an environment that encourages individuals to be themselves, however unique, so they can contribute and thrive.
INCLUSION ENABLERS	• Civility/Respect/Kindness Reference their individual definitions within this Glossary.

TERM	DEFINED
INTENT V. IMPACT	• Refers to problematic situations that often happen when people from different cultures communicate without being culturally competent. • The "Intent" is meant to be positive; however, the "Impact" is perceived as negative (Unintended Consequences).
KINDNESS	• Behavior marked by ethical characteristics, a pleasant disposition, and concern and consideration for others. It is considered a virtue and is recognized as a value in many cultures and religions. • The quality of being friendly, generous, and considerate. • *Extended Definition* ➤ Politeness is not the same as kindness. Being polite is what makes people feel good today. Being kind is doing what helps people get better tomorrow. In polite cultures, people withhold disagreement and criticism. In kind cultures, people speak their minds respectfully. ➤ "I'm just being honest" is a poor excuse for being rude. Candor is being forthcoming in what you say. Respect is being considerate in how you say it. Being direct with the content of your feedback doesn't prevent you from being thoughtful about the best way to deliver it. ➤ "I was just being myself" isn't an excuse for disrespectful behavior. It signals a lack of concern for others. Authenticity without empathy is selfish. Authenticity without boundaries is careless. Be true to your values but show regard for others' values.
NORMS	• Shared expectations within a given society about how members should behave and interact with one another.
OPPORTUNITY GAP/UNDER RESOURCED *(Underserved/ Marginalized)* **Communities People**	• "Systemically Marginalized." • Referring to the fact that the arbitrary circumstances in which people are born—such as their race, ethnicity, zip code, and socio-economic status—determine their opportunities in the educational system and life more broadly, rather than all people having the chance to achieve the best of their potential.

TERM	DEFINED
	• In business, a market opportunity that a company or individual is not addressing.
	• In politics, a euphemism for a lack of Equal Opportunity
	• Generally speaking, Opportunity Gap refers to inputs—the unequal or inequitable distribution of resources and opportunities.
	• Opportunity Gap and Under Resourced are the evolving terms replacing underserved and marginalized: evolving generational language.
ORGANIZATIONAL INTELLIGENCE	• Knowledge of what an organization is all about—an essential skill of a DEIB Leader.
	• A predicate for designing a DEIB Strategic Visioning Framework to ensure receptiveness.
	• The capability of an organization to comprehend and create knowledge relevant to its purpose; in words, it is the intellectual capacity of the entire organization. With relevant organizational intelligence comes great potential value for companies and organizations to discern where their strengths and weaknesses lie in responding to change and complexity.
	See Chapter 9 for additional information.
PERSON OF COLOR	• Usually used in place of the word "Minority" when referencing populations.
	• Refers to all Federal EEO classifications except White/Caucasian, non-Hispanic
	➤ African American/Black
	➤ American Indian/Alaskan (Indigenous)
	➤ Asian/Asian Indian
	➤ Hawaiian/Pacific Islander
	➤ Hispanic/Latino
	➤ Two or more Races

TERM	DEFINED
PRIVILEGE	• "Is when You think something is not a problem because it's not a problem to You, Personally!" ~David Gaider https://www.azquotes.com/author/40165-David_Gaider • "Forms of access to resources that result from legal or social norms having to do with membership in a group, usually without any particular action, inaction, or even awareness on the part of the people who have that access of the existence of the disparity, the potential benefits to them, or the costs to others." ~Miki Kashtan https://thefearlessheart.org/youre-not-a-bad-person-how-facing-privilege-can-be-liberating/ https://thefearlessheart.org/privilege-responsibility-and-nonviolence/
WHITE PRIVILEGE	• The phrase "White Privilege" refers to the social and economic advantages that White people have by virtue of the color of their skin in a culture in which the hue of your skin and racial inequality plays a significant role in how members of the culture interact.
RESPECT	• To treat with Consideration. Value. Regard. • To be kind; show courtesy. • To value the individual. • Respecting the individual needs, talents, and differences of those in the community.
REVERSE DISCRIMINATION	• A coined term with no legal significance that is sometimes used to characterize unlawful discrimination against a member of the majority—currently in the United States, Whites. • Unlawful discrimination is unlawful discrimination—whether the victim of discrimination is Black, White, Male, Female, Christian, Jewish, Muslim, Disabled, or Able-bodied.

TERM	DEFINED
SEGREGATION	• Broadly speaking, the action or state of setting someone or something apart from others. Within the context of DEIB and U.S. history, it refers to laws and practices requiring separate housing, education, job categories, and other services for Persons of Color, apart from those services provided for White People.
STRATEGIC VISIONING FRAMEWORK.	• A process that involves creating a clear, long-term, and aspirational picture of where an organization wants to be in the future, guiding its strategic planning, decision-making, and resource allocation to achieve that vision with metrics and accountability.
	• A Holistic DEIB Strategic Visioning Framework helps organizations define their desired forward-thinking state, providing a roadmap for long-term success by motivating the organization beyond its current capabilities with a Belonging Lens.
	• The DEIB Strategic Visioning Framework sequential alignment components:
	1. An Organization's Vision, Mission, Core Values, Purpose
	2. Pillars/Focus Areas with Objectives
	3. Prioritized Initiatives for each Pillar/Focus Area
	4. Implementation/Metrics/Accountability
	• Regular Reporting/Communication Timeframes
	Reference: Sequential Alignment Components in Chapter 7.
SWOT ANALYSIS W/DEIB LENS	• SWOT: Strength/Weakness/Opportunity/Threat
	• A structured planning method that evaluates these four elements of an organization, project, or business venture. A SWOT analysis can be carried out for a company, product, place, industry, or person. It involves specifying the objective of the business venture or project and identifying the internal and external factors that are favorable and unfavorable to achieve that objective.

TERM	DEFINED
	• A basic, analytical framework that assesses what an entity (usually a business, though it can be used for a place, industry or product) can and cannot do, for factors both internal (the strengths and weaknesses) as well as external (the potential opportunities and threats). Using environmental data to evaluate the position of a company, a SWOT analysis determines what assists the firm in accomplishing its objectives, and what obstacles must be overcome or minimized to achieve desired results: where the organization is today, and where it may be positioned in the future. • *Strengths:* Characteristics of the business/organization/agency or project that give it an advantage over others. ➢ What an organization excels at and separates it from the competition: things like a strong brand, loyal customer base, strong balance sheet, unique technology, specific information or results, for instance. • *Weaknesses:* Stops an organization from performing at its optimum level. They are areas where the business needs to improve to remain competitive and valued. ➢ Characteristics of the business/organization/agency that place the business or project at a disadvantage relative to others. • *Opportunities:* Refers to favorable external factors that an organization can use to give it a competitive advantage. ➢ Elements in the environment that the business/organization/agency or project could exploit or leverage to its advantage. • *Threats:* Elements in the internal and/or external environment that could cause trouble for the business/organization/agency or project. ➢ Referring to factors that have the potential to harm an organization.

TERM	DEFINED
SYSTEMIC CHANGE	Confronting root causes of issues (rather than symptoms) by transforming structures, customs, mindsets, power dynamics, and policies, by strengthening collective power through the active collaboration of diverse people and organizations. This collaboration is rooted in shared goals to achieve lasting improvement to solve problems at a local, national, and global level.
UNLAWFUL DISCRIMINATION	"Discrimination" is the act or instance of making a distinction. It can include the treatment or consideration of, or making a distinction in favor of or against, a person based on one or more Dimensions of Diversity, or upon the group, class, or category to which that person belongs. Unlawful discrimination occurs when the action is prohibited by a law, rule, regulation, court decision, or any other lawful authority.
WALK THE TALK	• Putting your words into action—showing that you mean what you say by actively modeling it yourself (practice what you preach). • Demonstrated Behaviors that reflect the entity's words—commitment to DEIB, mission, core values, policy, website messaging, recruiting/marketing message. Once you commit to something, stand by it.
WORKPLACE EXPECTATIONS	• Encompasses the assumed or stated behaviors, performance levels, and outcomes that both employers and employees anticipate from each other in a professional setting. • A trust driven by collaborative teamwork that everyone within the four walls of the organization will have behaviors that reflect the organization's vision, mission, and core values while enabling an inclusive and healthy work-life balance* environment. ➤ *Remember: It is unfair and a break in trust to hold someone accountable when expectations and consequences have not previously been clearly communicated.* **The term "work-life balance" was coined by Generation X in comparing previous generations of "workacholic" v. "work life balance." Generations after the Boomers now expect balanced time for: family, work, self (personal time) = mental health. Definitely part of DEIB end in mind of fostering a healthy belonging culture.*

TERM	DEFINED
WORLD VIEW	• A set of beliefs and assumptions that a person uses when interpreting the world around them. • A person's World View is shaped by what they have or have not been exposed to and/or experienced.

This Glossary is designed to be a frequent resource, now and in the future. We hope you'll use it to help your organization adopt a shared vocabulary to improve communications about and understanding of DEIB.

ABOUT THE AUTHORS

Deborah D. Vereen is a nationally recognized Strategic Thinker and DEIB Thought Leader, with over twenty-five years of experience driving systemic change across business, education, community, and government sectors. As the founder of THE VEREEN GROUP, she partners with executives and organizations to build sustainable cultures of belonging through practical strategies that foster equity, belonging, and leadership excellence aligned with their mission, vision, and core values.

A Cornell Certified Diversity Professional/Advanced Practitioner (CCDP/AP) and master facilitator, Deborah has designed and led transformative initiatives that integrate DEIB Principles into every facet of business operations. Her expertise in strategic planning, leadership coaching, discovery learning, and inclusionary metrics has made her a sought-after consultant, Forbes Expert Panel contributor, and a trusted voice in shaping human-centered leadership.

Recognized for her groundbreaking work, Deborah has received multiple awards, including the Business Diversity Champion Award, Human Relations Commission Corporate Citizenship Diversity Award, the Leadership in Diversity Award, and has been recognized as one of the most "Influential Inclusion Leaders." She has served on numerous boards, chaired and co-chaired inclusionary committees for organizations.

Driven by the belief that belonging is the foundation of progress, Deborah empowers leaders to cultivate workplaces where dignity, safety, and respect fuel meaningful success. Her work has guided executives, legislators, and organizations in navigating the evolving landscape of holistic leadership and inclusion. In 2008 she co-founded the Diversity and Inclusion Professionals of Central Pennsylvania as a professional development tool for Diversity and Inclusion Professionals. Deborah continues to champion progress, belonging, and sustainable forward-thinking transformation in organizations.

Deborah enjoys baking her famous cheesecake for family and friends while savoring a cup of tea, sunlight, and nature on her three-season porch in Pennsylvania.

Frank Miles grew up during the 1960s; his mother's support of the Civil Rights Movement made a lasting impression. After graduating from Bucknell University, where the subject of his honors thesis was the *Bakke* affirmative action case, he earned his *Juris Doctorate* from the George Washington University Law School.

After practicing for eighteen years with the region's largest law firm, Frank became Vice President, Secretary, and General Counsel of a major corporation, which had only recently hired its first Diversity Director. This was at a time when Diversity initiatives were just beginning to be undertaken by a handful of organizations.

As corporate secretary and strategic planning leader, Frank suggested that his position have oversight of Diversity efforts to underscore their importance to the entire enterprise. He was able to leverage his role throughout the community by encouraging his company to support fledgling projects like the local African American and LGBT Chambers of Commerce, and the Hispanic Community Center.

Frank has chaired, co-chaired, and been a member of DEIB committees at several organizations. In 2008 he co-founded the Diversity and Inclusion Professionals of Central Pennsylvania as a professional development tool for Diversity and Inclusion Professionals. His DEIB work has been recognized by a variety of organizations, including the Harrisburg Regional Chamber of Commerce and the Central Pennsylvania Gay and Lesbian Chamber of Commerce.

Frank resides with his wife of forty-five years on their Pennsylvania farm and enjoys the great good fortune of living within walking distance of their children and families.

The B Corp Movement

Dear reader,

Thank you for reading this book and joining the Publish Your Purpose community! You are joining a special group of people who aim to make the world a better place.

What's Publish Your Purpose About?

Our mission is to elevate the voices often excluded from traditional publishing. We intentionally seek out authors and storytellers with diverse backgrounds, life experiences, and unique perspectives to publish books that will make an impact in the world.

Beyond our books, we are focused on tangible, action-based change. As a woman- and LGBTQ+-owned company, we are committed to reducing inequality, lowering levels of poverty, creating a healthier environment, building stronger communities, and creating high-quality jobs with dignity and purpose.

Certified

Corporation

As a Certified B Corporation, we use business as a force for good. We join a community of mission-driven companies building a more equitable, inclusive, and sustainable global economy. B Corporations must meet high standards of transparency, social and environmental performance, and accountability as determined by the nonprofit B Lab. The certification process is rigorous and ongoing (with a recertification requirement every three years).

How Do We Do This?

We intentionally partner with socially and economically disadvantaged businesses that meet our sustainability goals. We embrace and encourage our authors and employee's differences in race, age, color, disability, ethnicity, family or marital status, gender identity or expression, language, national origin, physical and mental ability, political affiliation, religion, sexual orientation, socio-economic status, veteran status, and other characteristics that make them unique.

Community is at the heart of everything we do—from our writing and publishing programs to contributing to social enterprise nonprofits like reSET (https://www.resetco.org/) and our work in founding B Local Connecticut.

We are endlessly grateful to our authors, readers, and local community for being the driving force behind the equitable and sustainable world we are building together.

To connect with us online, or publish with us,
visit us at www.publishyourpurpose.com.

Elevating Your Voice,

Jenn T Grace

Jenn T. Grace
Founder, Publish Your Purpose